Be Unique or Be Ignored™
The CEO's Guide to Branding

Marc H. Rudov

MHR Enterprises
Brentwood, CA

Be Unique or Be Ignored™
The CEO's Guide to Branding

By Marc H. Rudov

Published by:
MHR Enterprises
P.O. Box 818
Brentwood, CA 94513-0818
MarcRudov.com

ISBN: 978-0-9745017-3-4 (paperback)
ISBN: 978-0-9745017-5-8 (eBook)

Library of Congress Data
Rudov, Marc H.,
    Be unique or be ignored: the CEO's guide to branding/Marc H.
    Rudov
    —1st ed.
    ISBN: 978-0-9745017-3-4 (paperback)
    1. Branding
    2. Marketing
    3. Sales
    4. Business strategy

Library of Congress Control Number: 2013920226

The lead car is unique, except for the one behind it, which is identical.

Murray Walker
The Voice of Formula One Racing

To my dear Claudia, who made this possible.

Table of Contents

PREFACE

Why a guide to branding for you, the CEO? Here's why: Your brand is *directly* tied to your revenue growth and profitability. Branding is critical to your company's success, whether it's in the commercial, consumer, defense, education, healthcare, industrial, or technology sector.

Ultimately, branding is *your* responsibility—not that of your marketing department, PR firms, ad agencies, Facebook, or Twitter. Odds are, your brand's weak. You **must** know why!

I've cringed numerous times at a CEO's *four-paragraph* response to a TV or magazine reporter's standard question: "Exactly what business is your company in?" Such a verbose, nebulous, forgettable oration—*which should be one sentence, delivered within 15 seconds*—signifies branding failure.

Every successful trial lawyer will aver that the key to victory in any courtroom, in any case, is "grabbing" the jurors—*in their language*—during the first 15 seconds of his opening statement. Your brand is your opening statement.

Go to your company's homepage. Put your hand over the logo and company name. Now, identify that company. I'll bet you can't, because your homepage looks and reads like every competitor's homepage: filled with jargon and generic boilerplate. More evidence of branding failure. Your company is blending, not branding; ubique, not unique; dwelling in the white noise of me-too competition—a universal problem and the reason I call myself The WhiteNoise Doctor™.

Branding is the CEO's #1 priority. Your brand is akin to an arrowhead: if it isn't sharp, the arrow won't stick in its target. Every repeated attempt to shoot that dull-tipped arrow into the target is a costly resource-waster. The smart, effective solution: Sharpen that brand, so that it sticks the first time.

Analogously, your brand is the proverbial stone in the pond, begetting multiple concentric ripples. *All* other business functions—especially engineering, capital-raising, marketing, and sales—depend on and emanate from the brand. But, if your company is typical, there's a good chance that branding incorrectly *follows* product development. It's an afterthought. This common error is like creating a blueprint *after* erecting a skyscraper. Who does *that*?

The brand *is* your company's reputation, and vice versa. It dictates your costs of sales, capital, and media. If people don't "get" your brand—*your value proposition*—within 15 seconds, they'll resist purchasing from, investing in, and writing about your firm. Or, they'll ignore it altogether. Hence, the title of this guide: Be Unique or Be Ignored™.

Yet, to my neverending surprise and chagrin, I find that most CEOs don't understand branding, and don't want to understand it—they delegate, or relegate, it to others—or they simply don't care about it. To them, branding is a low-priority, esoteric, delayable (or avoidable) task. *They tell me this!*

Furthermore, too often the CEO deems branding a bunch of fluff, so obviously easy that every texting junkie with a Twitter account is an expert at it. I've seen such dismissive CEOs solicit "opinions" about branding, under the politically correct guise of teamwork, from unqualified individuals—or worse, that dysfunctional *branding committee*—resulting in useless, unfathomable junk. Sound familiar?

It's bad enough when people outside the building can't fathom your brand. It's worse when the people *inside* it—your employees—are befuddled. Believe me: they are.

Ask your receptionist, head of HR, and engineering and sales VPs why your company exists, *why it's unique.* Do they stammer and give you cloudy, jargonized responses?

Finally, the antithesis of brand is commodity. If your brand is indistinguishable from those of your competitors, you are selling a commodity; customers will treat it and buy it accordingly—if they notice it at all. Is that what you want?

This guide for CEOs will disabuse you of conventional thinking and misconceptions, and convince you to end failing practices and **make branding *your* #1 priority**.

MARC H. RUDOV
November 2013
Bay Area, CA

CHAPTER ONE

Branding Basics

Branding is an age-old identification practice, traced back to the Ancient Egyptians, which livestock owners use to permanently mark their herds. The "brand," usually a symbol or code, is burned, frozen, tattooed, or tagged onto an animal. It has no *inherent* meaning other than distinguishing its owner and his livestock from other livestock and their owners, in cases of lost or stolen animals.

Marketers metaphorically have adapted this livestock branding to the business world, to differentiate their companies and products from those of their competitors. Instead of hot irons, they employ words, images, and sounds to make lasting "impressions" on customers, investors, media pros, analysts, and other influencers.

Branding has two components: the message and the megaphone (the branding platforms): homepage, tradeshows, CEO keynotes, radio/TV interviews, salesforce, sales training, product/corporate brochures, financial documents, industry and financial analysts, IPO roadshows, advertising, PR, joint ventures, partnering, articles, and social media.

Alas, most companies emphasize the megaphone and minimize the message, believing that incessant social-media posting and search-engine optimization somehow compensate for nebulosity. Look around; it's true. **Reality:** Sending white noise through a megaphone generates louder white noise.

It gets worse. Companies habitually nurse inconsistent and out-of-synch branding platforms, each one featuring a different message! Example: your salesreps and homepage tell completely different stories. Totally unacceptable.

At MarcRudov.com, I conducted a poll of 800 senior-level exec, as well as salesreps, with this question: *According to YOUR SALESREPS, how helpful to successfully closing business is YOUR company's homepage?* The results didn't shock me: 38% of respondents voted "saleskiller"; 27% voted "irrelevant"; only 13% voted "extremely helpful." What does all this mean? **CEOs are wasting marketing dollars**. Not good.

How can you, the CEO, expect customers, investors, analysts, and reporters to form a crystal-clear, unique feel for your company when you broadcast confusing and conflicting signals to them? Hint: you can't. White noise is costly!

Brand/Commodity Battle

We appreciate a person who gets to "the point" quickly, succinctly, and memorably—a unique standout who's never confused with others. We gravitate to him *because he adds maximum value, at minimum cost, to our lives.* We know what he stands for, and we can describe it easily. Ronald Reagan was that kind of man. He had a unique brand that endures.

Likewise, we gravitate to a vendor that gets to "the point" quickly, succinctly, memorably: *We know your problem, have a unique solution, and urge you to act now.* Never do we confuse a unique vendor with its jargon-spewing, white-noise-dwelling rivals, which force us to play eenie meenie miny moe.

A brand is *not* a jargonized, functional description of your product; it *is* your value proposition, your billboard, your opening statement, your barcode, your reason d'être, the jar that exposes your jam. Products and technologies change every six months, but a strong brand outlives both.

The first benefit of having a strong brand is the ability to charge a premium over your competitors' prices (and your costs). Why? Your customers believe that you offer unique value, *expressed in their language*, vis-a-vis your competitors.

Alternatively, the more you look and sound like your rivals—*your customers can't distinguish you from them*—the more your product resembles a commodity and, thus, must succumb to commodity pricing: *no premium.* Using jargon assures your company of commodity status.

Your neverending battle is crystal-clear: fight against becoming a commodity. If branding is *not* your #1 priority, you *will* lose this battle—I guarantee it.

Brand Dictates Cost of Sales

The second benefit of a strong brand is a lower cost of sales. Is your sales cycle—the time from identifying a prospect to closing the deal—one year or greater? If so, you have a costly sales cycle: endless calls, emails, faxes, overnighted parcels, face-to-face meetings, teleconferences, spinning your wheels, and insanity.

Have you asked yourself why it takes your company at least 12 months to close a sale? Any CEO worth his salt has pondered this challenge. Perhaps your product is lackluster, or you employ an ineffective salesforce or channel. But, without knowing you or your company, I'll tell you why your cost of sales is unnecessarily high: *your brand is weak.*

In Chapter 14, "Always Be Branding," I list the top-five excuses CEOs invariably give me for avoiding or delaying branding activity. I'll repeat them here:

1. We're too busy for that
2. Our company is too small
3. It's not a priority right now
4. It's too expensive
5. We did that last year.

Newsflash: Brand dictates cost of sales—*regardless of your company's size, age, or industry!* Branding is necessity, not luxury.

As I will repeat incessantly throughout this guide, a strong brand is a *unique* articulation of a company's value proposition (AKA its marketing message, its raison d'être, its barcode, its opening statement). It elicits emotions, always, *regardless of company size, age, or industry*, and is expressed *succinctly and memorably in customer-centric language.*

Time is the brand's enemy: the longer it takes to explain a value proposition, the less value it has; the more it contains product-centric language, ditto that. Consequently, the longer it takes people to remember and repeat a brand, *if they do*, the higher its cost. As seen in the hourglass metaphor below: more sand spilled, more brand killed. **A weak brand wastes time and maximizes the cost of sales.**

Customers, investors, reporters, and analysts easily, quickly **react** to, **remember**, and **repeat** a strong brand (note the apex of the messaging pyramid below). At this apex—your target—the sales cycle is short, the cost of sales low.

A strong brand gets to the point (pun intended), fast. A weak brand slowly or never gets to the point and inhabits the cold basement. Intuitive, is it not? No spreadsheets required.

Choice: invest in a strong brand or keep wasting cash on a bloated salesforce and unfathomable, unmemorable ads.

Brand Determines Decisionmaker

In the previous section, we discussed length of sales cycle and how it escalates the *cost* of sales. This protracted sales cycle always afflicts jargon-junkie, high-tech vendors, and they never seem to understand the root cause. High-tech vendors are usually founded by engineers, who eat, drink, sleep, and breathe jargon. They know no other language and believe the rest of us are kindred spirits. They're wrong.

When you employ jargon—on your homepage, in your sales pitches, and everywhere else—only the customer's geeks understand it. This disaster wreaks three problems: 1) your product screams "commodity"; 2) the geeks have to put your product through their lengthy "evaluation" process, *if they feel like it*; and 3) geeks control the purchase decision. Nightmare!

Oracle was famous in its infancy for selling database software to *CEOs and boards of directors*, who then delegated implementation to their IT folks. EMC Corporation likewise grew rapidly selling *storage systems* to top execs, *not IT*, by using *business lingo*, not technojargon. See a pattern here?

Three Steps to Branding Success

To succeed in branding, you must articulate a *unique*, concise message, *in customer language,* that the audience "gets" within 15 seconds. *Jargonized vendorspeak is totally unacceptable:* **Never** mention your product, product features, or technology in your brand, or value proposition. Never.

A value proposition is just that: an articulation of value (benefits) to customers, who focus on *their* lives, not yours. Customers buy *benefits*, not products. Vendors exist to solve customers' problems, or grant their wishes, and, therefore, must convey via branding messages the relief or fantasy, respectively, they're delivering to customers—*in customer language.* CEOs have a hard time with this concept: They tend to default to generic jargon (e.g., cloud computing), which is antithetical to unique customer language. Jargon is a lazy crutch that helps CEOs feel safe, hip, and part of the "industry club"—but is why their companies look and sound alike and dwell in the white noise of me-too competition.

Three Steps to Branding Success

Your unique, 15-second message must adhere to my three R's: *react, remember,* and *repeat.* If your target audience does not *react emotionally* to your message, it has failed. If they do not *remember* your message, it has failed. Finally, if they do not *repeat* your message, which won't happen if your message doesn't meet the first two conditions, it has failed.

How often have you left a meeting with a vendor, forgetting what you heard just 20 minutes earlier? On the other hand, you still remember Ronald Reagan urging Mikhail Gorbachev to "tear down this wall," don't you?

The Logo Isn't a Brand

In addition to the message, a key tool of branding is the logo, an identification symbol designed to represent its owner. Logo derives from the Greek word *logos,* whose primary definition is *meaning.* You'll likely recall the famous psychiatrist Viktor Frankl, exemplified in every success book, who described his survival from a Nazi concentration camp in *Man's Search for Meaning.* From this book, he invented a new branch of psychiatry called logotherapy, whose central tenet is that finding meaning in life is everyone's chief motivator—and that *each person must choose and create this meaning.*

Consistent with Frankl and contrary to conventional thinking, a logo is *not* a brand and has no inherent meaning. In fact, a marketer must create the brand *before* affixing its visible representation, the logo, on anything. Unfortunately, many seriously believe that hiring a firm to redesign the logo constitutes rebranding the company. It most certainly does not! The brand is a value proposition, not a picture. *The logo can represent a brand but never constitute one.*

An organization can use the same logo for years, even though its meaning changes drastically over time: worse or better business practices, varying financial results, new target markets, and shifting audience perceptions.

In rare cases, companies have excelled so brilliantly at branding that their unique logos are universally recognized and understood for the values they represent. To wit: Apple's brand is now so strong, its bitten-pome logo, displayed sans company name, amply conveys Apple's cool-lifestyle message.

Here's an example of what I'll call brandshift, where the brand, the value proposition, underlying the logo has changed over time: Dove skin and beauty products from Unilever. According to Unilever, Dove introduced the beauty bar for women in 1957. For 53 years, Dove and its logo, and its products, have meant one thing: women.

Then, in 2010, Unilever went unisex. It launched a line of skin products for men, under the Dove® Men+Care® rubric, while *using the same logo!* This gambit represents a huge shift in catering to the male's self-image, attitudes, and habits—his willingness to use products associated with femininity. Here's a Dove ad for the Russian market (the same ad appeared in many markets), depicting a macho man pampering his skin.

Considering the rise of the "metrosexual," a male who primps and preens like a woman, this brand extension isn't a surprise. Gillette (T*he Best a Man Can Get*), by the way, did the opposite: it created Venus razors and Satin Care gels and moisturizers for women. I don't agree with Unilever's blurry Dove strategy. Its young-male-targeted line of AXE personal-care products makes much more sense.

The second example of brandshift, as seen in the next figure, is the logo of the USA: the presidential seal. Let's face it: The perception of America, both inside and outside the country, is worse than it was 50 years ago. Its value literally and figuratively has declined:

- $17T in unpayable debt
- Antibusiness climate
- Tyrannical utopian government, including takeover and destruction of healthcare
- Humiliating Healthcare.gov "rollout"
- Diminished personal wealth
- Defanged military
- Russia and China thumbing their noses at us
- Growing terrorism
- Rampant unemployment, runaway addiction to disability, foodstamps, and other social programs.

What Is a Brand
Value Proposition – *NOT* a logo

OLD BRAND
- Power
- Prosperity
- Pride
- Liberty

NEW BRAND
- Impotence
- Insolvency
- Inferiority
- Fascism

SAME LOGO

WhiteNoise

MarcRudov.com
© 2010 Marc Rudov

The USA is no longer the feared, respected, admired, prosperous, liberty-loving, free-enterprise superpower it used to be. Same logo, though. Would a new logo help? No way. The USA's broken brand—its value proposition—must be fixed.

Finally, let's consider the unusual case of replacing a logo, under duress, while maintaining the same corporate brand. In the 1850s, Procter & Gamble (P&G), which today is a purveyor of 50 brands—including Gillette, Tide, Pampers, and Crest products—created a logo depicting the Man-in-the-Moon (MITM) staring at 13 stars, which represented the 13 colonies. In the 1980s, rumors began to fly that the horns in the hair and the upside-down 666s in the beard of P&G's MITM represented Satan (1st image). This battle continued for almost a decade. P&G simplified that logo in 1991 (2nd image), failing to quell the controversy. Later in 1991, P&G adopted a completely new logo (3rd image), ending the ordeal. In 2013, P&G modified its logo with new font and hint of moon sliver (4th image). How much does all this matter to P&G's brand?

I contend that, despite the controversy and the money wasted to kill it, few people know or care about P&G's new logo, or its history. Ask your friends if they recall P&G's old

MITM logo. You'll mostly get shoulder shrugs. To be fair, we know P&G's products—Tide Crest, Cascade, Gillette, Braun, etc.—better than the parent corporation, P&G. In fact, we don't know P&G that well.

Just as a logo isn't a brand, neither is a product or a product name a brand. That's right: *Only a value proposition is a brand.* If potential customers know your product name but not *why* it's unique and desirable, there's no brand. Howard Schultz, CEO of Starbucks, told *Fortune* magazine, for the 12.12.11 issue: *"We're not in the coffee business—we're in the experience business."*

Don't get me wrong; a logo isn't a waste of money—a unique logo is always beneficial, a murky logo not. But, remember this: a logo *represents* the brand, never constitutes it! At the product and corporate levels, your brands, your value propositions, which live in the *guts* of customers, investors, analysts, and reporters, are paramount. *Guts?* Yes, guts. Read the next chapter.

CHAPTER TWO

B2B: Branding to Business

After deeming yet another technology firm's homepage incomprehensible, I received a mind-numbingly incompetent response from its founder: "*Branding?* Why? Who cares? Do you realize we're in the B2B [business-to-business] space?"

Let me translate her unfortunately typical response:

1. Our Website, which nobody reads, merely exists to spew jargon, validate our company's existence and importance, and catalog our products

2. I've never worked on commission and have no clue about the art of rapport-building and relationship-based selling

3. I'm unschooled in human behavior, face-to-face communications, and the emotions of corporate purchasing

4. Branding, whatever that is, is for consumers—so I've been told

5. Corporate buyers are unemotional spreadsheet robots, willing to inconvenience themselves by:

o   demanding, then poring through, lots of data sheets

o   wasting time watching our corporate videos and reading our white papers

o   hunting for and surmising the essence of our company and its product

o   after all the heavy lifting, "logically" purchasing the desired product.

Such ineptitude *is* typical, the primary reason almost every homepage within an industry looks like every other homepage in that industry: a generic jargon-junkyard, bereft of compelling, customer-centric messaging. Let's face it: Poor communication is amazingly acceptable and widespread in the business world—it's not a coincidence that so many execs dismiss and eschew B2B branding, unwittingly escalating their costs of sales, capital, and media.

The acronym B2B means *business-to-business* and encompasses the activities of companies peddling their wares to other businesses (vs. to consumers). Uninformed execs believe that branding to businesses is oxymoronic. They couldn't be more wrong.

As I already have done and will continue to repeat ad nauseam, branding supersedes *all* other business activities; it's your *first* priority, regardless of your industry or customer category or company size. CEOs who forget or disregard this axiom, and boards that don't demand that it be obeyed, will pay—big time. To wit:

> Meg Whitman, who grew eBay to prominence and lost her bid to run California, took the reins of HP in 2011. In the second paragraph of a *NYT* article by Quentin Hardy, we read: *"She has been chief executive of Hewlett-Packard for a little more than a year, and many people are still waiting for her to get her message out about the place."*

> This is called branding failure. In fact, later in the article, we read: *"HP spends $4B a year on marketing, and, according to an arm of the ad agency WPP, has one of the fastest-eroding brands among major companies."*

Do you remember when leftist lunatics roundly criticized Mitt Romney for saying, in the 2012 presidential race, that corporations are people? Of course, Romney was right. Apple Computer, without the return of founder Steve Jobs, would have died in 1997.

Even Jack Welch, former CEO of General Electric, had to opine his incredulity, in a 2012 *Wall Street Journal* editorial, "It's True: Corporations Are People," at the absurdity of anyone questioning that corporations are people:

> *This fact is so obvious that there can only be one conclusion ... when we hear the pronouncement, "Corporations aren't people"—that it's doublespeak.*

That is, when people say that corporations aren't people, what they really want to say is, "Business is evil."

Who makes payroll, profits, and purchases? Who creates powerful messaging? Could it be bricks, glass, steel, machines, and stock? No, people perform such "logical" tasks—with three fundamental business emotions influencing them at all times: *power, reputation, and paycheck.*

Branding to business (B2B) is the art and science of articulating a value proposition, in jargon-free language, that succinctly, uniquely, and memorably captures one or all of the three business emotions. A brand's purpose is to persuade business people to buy from, invest in, and write about your company. Here's what a brand is *not*: a jargon-laced, functional description of your product.

What does this mean? If your homepage features a picture of your product—described as "the fastest, cheapest, smallest widget in the world"—you're not branding.

B2B branding is *not* oxymoronic; it's essential to your company's success. Whether directed to business execs or consumers, branding is communicating. Poor or nonexistent communication is at the core of every failed relationship, business and personal, is it not?

Your homepage is the leading indicator of your brand's strength: If it sucks, if it reads like a nutrition label, if your top salesperson doesn't use it as a tool to close a sale, your brand sucks.

Conversely, your brand is stellar and strong you're your target audiences:

- "Get it" in 15 seconds
- REACT to, REMEMBER, and REPEAT its unique, concise value proposition
- Don't ask you to explain, once again, what your company does/sells.

Corporations *are* people, whose business emotions may differ from their at-home emotions—but their decisions, in all realms, are always driven by emotions. Ignore them at your peril.

Remember: B2B is branding to business.

CHAPTER THREE

GutShare™ vs. Mindshare

In the preceding chapter, I presented my three R's of branding, the first of which is: *If your target audience does not react emotionally to your message, it has failed.*

I will tell you that many CEOs and their underlings, in the industrial and high-tech sectors, reject and dismiss such "heresy," believing instead that corporate buyers are logical spreadsheet jockeys, while only consumers make emotional decisions. These execs couldn't be more wrong, as if they've never sold anything before! Not surprisingly, their ubiquitous homepages, which *should* be their best sales tools, are, in fact, as enticing as nutrition labels.

David Kelley, founder of IDEO, one of the world's top industrial-design firms, told *Fortune* magazine (04.29.13) his philosophy of human behavior: *"Nothing in life is done with one side of the brain. Everything has an emotional content and a pragmatic aspect."*

Exactly, Mr. Kelley. And, anyone who tries to engage in cerebral persuasion—whether in person, on the phone, or through a homepage—will fail. Nobody buys cerebrally.

As you examine your life, what stands out most about the victories, failures, paramours, jobs, bosses, songs, movies, family, paintings, vacations, homes, and cars from that life? Is it your intellectual deductions? No, it's the emotions.

Exceptional events, places, people, and possessions make *visceral* impacts on your *gut*—the nexus between, and confluence of, your mind and heart. Your gut is the true barometer of your memories, reactions, and anticipations. When you've made a good decision, how do you know? You *feel* it in your gut. Correspondingly, when you've made a bad decision, how do you know? You *feel* it in your gut. Literally.

Watch Tiger Woods hit a tee-shot. When it's perfect, he immediately bends down to pick up his tee, without ever watching his ball in flight, and begins walking to the fairway. Meanwhile, the TV camera has been trained on the shot from beginning to end. How does Tiger know, without looking and analyzing, that he executed perfectly? He can *feel it* in his gut.

When a person has a big decision to make, he typically likes to sleep on it. Why? During sleep, the whole body will process that decision, culling data from mind and heart. Upon rising the next morning, the decisionmaker can *feel* the right answer in his gut, where his body places it. Unfortunately, all too often, we ignore our guts. Anyone who's married the wrong spouse or accepted the wrong job offer, when the gut clearly warned against it, acutely grasps this phenomenon.

Malcolm Gladwell wrote *Blink: The Power of Thinking Without Thinking,* a bestselling book about rapid cognition, making decisions based on what occurs in the first two seconds of any situation. Overthinking always takes one away from the solution his gut knows is right. *Blink* validates the gut as a powerful decisionmaking instrument.

Donald Trump had to decide which candidate to fire each week on *The Apprentice,* or which one to hire at the end of 13 weeks. He began each series with a slew of highly accomplished executives, who looked amazing on paper. Prior to getting an in-person "feel" for them, he couldn't discern one from the other. Trump often struggled with his personnel decisions but ultimately admitted trusting his gut every time.

Every CEO must decide with imperfect or inadequate data. The only way to fill the "info gap" is by using his gut, thereby taking a risk (*an emotional move*). He can't be an effective executive without trusting his gut.

GutShare™
© 2009 by Marc H. Rudov
MarcRudov.com

In August 2010, David L. Sokol shared with *Fortune* magazine what he then considered his biggest business failure. In the early 2000s, he invested in a new method to remove zinc from one of MidAmerican's geothermal wells in California. The technology worked in the lab, but, when applied in the field, it flopped, leaving MidAmerican with a $200M loss. In retrospect, Sokol should have done more pilot-testing:

> *"The worst mistake I made was that, when I approved the project, in the pit of my stomach, I knew it was a mistake. I've tried to teach this to young executives ever since: Your gut instincts are extremely important to listen to, particularly when they are telling you not to do something."*

The Hub of Buyer Behavior

The gut grows in power over time. The gut of a 25-year-old, who has little life experience, is no match for that of a 50-year-old. Because the gut combines and processes data from the mind and the heart, it is only as good as the weaker of those two organs. Nevertheless, the gut *is* what people use to make decisions, good or bad. Accordingly, their *guts* are what marketers must occupy to sell them products.

Question: If the gut is our chief decisionmaking tool, why is so much ink and time devoted to the mind? Countless books, articles, seminars, and business strategies are based on *mindshare,* that portion of space in the customer's *mind* that a vendor's product occupies.

Answer: I'll give you three reasons for the mindshare obsession in the business world:

1. People *feel* safer and more comfortable—ironically, pure emotion—justifying their business decisions in "conventional terms." In a *Business Week* piece (04.23.12), Venessa Wong cites evidence that people don't speak their minds at work: they're *blenders, not branders* (they like to fit in and loathe standing out). A Google search of mindshare yields over 1M listings—a lot of fealty to an accepted concept that ignores the essence of buyer behavior

2. Most employees, including those in marketing, never have sold before and know little, if anything, about buyers' emotions and motives. They really believe that purchasing decisions are cerebral; their jargon-laced messaging proves it

3. Companies, especially those in high-tech, have a proclivity to worship their products and product features—I call this disease *technologica erotica*. They're convinced that customers, investors, and reporters share this disease: *If you don't grasp our products, you need more data, more jargon!* Wrong.

The hub of buyer behavior is the gut, whether those buyers are residential, commercial, industrial, military, or scientific. Buyers of all stripes make gut-based decisions. So, the marketer who can resonate a customer's gut, as a stringed bow resonates a violin, will sell her a lot of products and services.

Yet, the preoccupation with mindshare persists. It is a mistake. Just as you can't win a prize at the carnival without hitting and sticking the target, you can't win a customer without hitting and sticking the target: his *gut*.

I have lots of product names stuck in my head—from a deluge of endless print, Internet, TV, and radio advertising—but this deluge of information overwhelms and bores me. The *only* product names that matter are the ones that *move* me, the ones stuck in my *gut*.

Because one advertiser outspends its rivals on TV spots, its product might occupy the most share of my mind. So what? Without moving me, though, I'm not going to buy the product—*unless it's the cheapest of the lot* (in other words, a commodity). I have, many times, bought the highest-priced product in a category because its vendor moved me, earning the biggest share of my *gut*.

Grabbing GutShare™

The true measure of branding effectiveness is the ability to grab GutShare™, that portion of the customer's *gut* one's product or service occupies. GutShare is what makes certain brands—those of Apple, BMW, Burberry, Comedy Central, ESPN, Fox News Channel, GE, Google, IBM, Intel, Louis Vuitton, Mercedes-Benz, Michelin, Rolex, Starbucks,

Tide, Tiffany, the *Wall Street Journal*, Windex, Walt Disney, and YouTube—break through the white noise to stand out.

The secret of grabbing GutShare? Piquing customers with the "right" message: a balance of logic and emotion (mind and heart) that resonates in their guts. *Chasing mindshare is a wasted focus—it will fail, and, therefore, is not branding.*

It takes guts to go for the gut—to buck convention by grabbing GutShare—while your lemming competitors fight futilely for mindshare. But, hitting *any* target doesn't win the prize; it must be the *right* target. Moreover, hitting the target isn't enough: the message must *stick* in the target, the gut. Whoever wins the most GutShare wins the customer.

Corporate Emotions

Every corporate decision is an emotional one, from hiring to purchasing to selecting meeting attendees. Recall the maxim from most of the 20th century: *Nobody ever got fired for buying IBM.* Sounds like fear to me. Last time I checked, fear is an emotion. In fact, IBM was famous for teaching its salesreps to use the FUD (fear, uncertainty, and doubt) sales technique. *Emotional selling to IT execs?* You betcha.

Let's simplify. There are three corporate emotions:
- **Power**
- **Reputation**
- **Paycheck.**

Every decision you make, *every* decision your direct reports make, *every* decision the customers, investors, and reporters make, is about *power* or *reputation* or *paycheck*—or any two of them or all three of them. If your product malfunctions or proves inferior at a customer's factory, the exec who approved its purchase may lose her job **(paycheck)**, get demoted **(power)**, or become known as the company bozo **(reputation)**. *Avoiding these painful emotions* is a huge driver of *every* corporate decision: purchase, product, personnel, etc.

If emotions play such a big role in buying, why do your marketers continue to ignore them when messaging? Why the focus on mindshare instead of GutShare? We answered this a few sections ago: *people are blenders; they crave fitting in.*

Look at your company's homepage, brochures, videos, and presentations. Listen to your salesreps' pitches. What do you find? A veritable sea of buzzwords, vernacular, jargon, argot, and vendorspeak—all bereft of buyer emotion. Isn't this what we call a disconnect? A disconnect with buyers, yes. A disconnect with fellow sheepish blenders, no.

In 2011, Daniel Hannan, British member of the European Parliament, published an alarming book about the decay of America, *The New Road to Serfdom*. In it, he opined about blender Americans:

> *"One by one, the differences are being ironed out. The US is Europeanizing its health system, tax take, daycare, welfare rules, approach to global warming, foreign policy, federal structure, unemployment rate. Perhaps Americans are keen to fit in. Perhaps they feel awkward about being the odd man out."*

In 1975, Ronald Reagan made a seminal speech at the Conservative Political Action Conference (CPAC). He warned his audience, in this passage, about blending:

> *"I don 't know about you, but I am impatient with those Republicans who after the last election rushed into print saying, "We must broaden the base of our party"—when what they meant was to fuzz up and blur even more the differences between ourselves and our opponents."*

Allan Bloom, in 1987, nailed the source of blending in his landmark book, *The Closing of the American Mind:*

> *"The great democratic danger, according to Tocqueville, is enslavement to public opinion. The claim of democracy is that every man decides for himself ... The active presence of a tradition in a man's soul* [religion, etiquette, the US Constitution, wisdom] *gives him a resource against the ephemeral, the kind of resource that only the wise can find can find simply within themselves. The*

paradoxical result of the liberation of reason is greater reliance on public opinion for guidance, a weakening of independence."

My Cousin Vinny is one of the best movies of all time. Two college buddies, Bill Gambini and Stan Rothenstein, are arrested in Wazoo, Alabama, for a murder they didn't commit. Vincent Gambini (Joe Pesci), a lawyer-cousin from Brooklyn sans litigation experience, arrives in town with girlfriend Lisa (Marisa Tomei) in tow to defend and free the two boys. Here's a snippet of dialogue between Vinny and Lisa, upon arrival in Wazoo. Lisa, dressed in typical outlandish Brooklyn garb, was cracking her gum and snapping photos on a cheap camera:

Vinny: *You stick out like a sore thumb around here.*
Lisa: *Me!?! What about you?*
Vinny: *I fit in better than you. At least I'm wearing cowboy boots.*
Lisa: *Oh, yeah, you blend.*

This social desire to blend, to fit in, not to stand out, is what has driven so much of our behavior since childhood. The pressure to conform comes from parents, teachers, clergy, TV, magazines, bosses, movies, politicians, and each other.

Look at kids in school. They all feel pressure to dress the same; think the same; listen to the same music; and use the same, like, broken English. To a certain extent, kids never outgrow the herd mentality, as Vinny and Lisa demonstrated.

That's precisely why so many companies are stuck in the white noise, where one is indistinguishable from the other:

CEOs project personal fears of standing out, personal desires to blend in, onto their employees. Hence, jargon runs amok.

>   **Rudov's Rule:** *You can brand or blend, but you can't do both. Make up your mind.*

You, the CEO, must fight your "blending impulse" and that of your staff, because it *will* dilute your brand. *Branding and blending are mutually exclusive.* Standing out from the white noise of me-too competition might rattle your comfort zone, but that's what it takes to excite customers, investors, reporters, and analysts.

Branding or Debranding?

Are you branding or *debranding*? Here's an easy test.

If you are branding, you're appealing to buyers' guts, where they make their purchase decisions. If you're appealing to their intellects, however, you're blending, or *debranding*.

If you're blending, or fitting in, you are not branding—you are *debranding*. That's right, debranding. Using industry jargon? You're definitely not branding—you're *debranding*. If you're chasing mindshare, you are *debranding*.

Any time you camouflage your value proposition with vendor language and industry jargon, you are debranding—blending into the grass like a hidden lion. This kills profitable growth. Is that your goal? I didn't think so. Yet, if you are honest, all your verbal and written communications contain vendor language and jargon.

Blending Into the Grass?

Jargon camouflages your brand and kills profitable growth.

Stop Jargonizing.
Stop Blending.
Start Branding.

© 2012 MarcRudov.com

Shortly after Apple's Steve Jobs died in October 2011, an optometrist promoted Steve's wire-rimmed eyeglasses with the headline: *Do You Wanna Look Like Steve?* My first reaction was one of repulsion. But, then, I thought about it. Of course! Most people are joiners, followers, and copycats: *blenders*. The optometrist's strategy made total sense: appeal to those who live for Facebook's "like" button, play Farmville, and join the "please-track-me" site, Foursquare—the same people always put in charge of branding (debranding) at their companies!

Blenders **Are *Not* Branders**

foursquare

FARMVILLE

Like

CHAPTER FOUR

Producing or Marketing?

Not a day goes by without a business article in (fill-in-the-blank) publication erroneously equating a product with a market. There's no excuse for this. I constantly see references to nonexistent wireless, mobile, smartphone, and cleantech markets, to name a few. *None* of these is a market. Not one.

Wireless, smartphone, and cleantech are technology and product categories—*not markets*—and such inexcusable confusion is equal in egregiousness to an accountant blithely mislabeling assets as liabilities, a doctor interchanging vein and artery. A market is comprised of *people*, not things, and this is immutable.

In 1989, I wrote "The Mystery of Marketing" to address this very issue. It stands as proof that nothing has changed in 25 years. If the definition of market is neither universally understood nor specifically fixed (it isn't), its derivative term, market*ing*, is, obviously, equally murky.

People commonly use "market" to denote a store that sells food, an exchange to trade stocks and bonds, a product category, a technology category, a country, an inventory of available jobs (the job market), and buyers of a product. One word *cannot* and *does not* have this many definitions!

This linguistic faux pas—repeated endlessly in books, seminars, boardrooms, business articles, TV programs, sales training, etc.—is the root of branding failure. Am I off-base? Tell a judge that arguments and statements are synonymous.

Your Product Is Not a Market

The biggest branding/marketing mistake your firm is making right now, because not one employee understands the true definitions of market and marketing, is product worship. Look at your homepage: *product worship*. All your messaging, both verbal and written, to employees and the external world, is product-centric. You are *producting*, not marketing.

Let's clarify the terminology. There are three entities in commerce; they are *not* interchangeable:

- **Industry (supply side)**
- **Market (demand side)**
- **Marketplace (interface/nexus).**

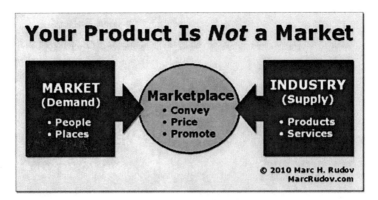

Industry is the *supply*, or business, side of the equation; it contains the vendors, products, services, channel partners, and technologies. There is a competitive industry. And, an industry can be crowded—until the weak players quit or consolidate.

Market is the *demand* side of the equation; it contains paying customers: people, not products or technologies. There's no such thing as a "competitive" or "crowded" market, despite what you'll read in the trade and business press: Customers don't fight each other over vendors!

Marketplace is the interface, or nexus, where the industries and markets meet to exchange value.

If I use a wireless product, don't call me a wireless customer, and don't lump me into a wireless market that doesn't exist. "Wireless" is nothing more than the enabling technology du jour that allows me to get my data, untethered.

For you to associate me with your product or technology label, just because I use it, is the epitome of hubris. I don't care about wireless—other than what it can do to ease life's challenges. If there's a better solution tomorrow, I'll take it.

Does this mean that the market of impatient, data-hungry consumers, of which I am a part, will have changed? Absolutely not. But, if you, the CEO, interchange product and market—as most people do—you will think so. This mistake *will* lead to lousy branding, the arrowhead of marketing.

Anyone who equates market and product will focus on the *product*—that's the essence of producting—and constantly miss opportunities to identify, serve, and gain sustainable loyalty from the market: customers. This, in turn, will beget suboptimal revenues and profits. It's just common sense.

Before Samsung's impressive rise, when Steve Jobs was alive, Apple understood this well, which explains why its loyal customers camped out overnight to buy iPhones.

Teaching the correct terminology to your employees, *and enforcing it*, will lead to a significant and rapid rise in your brand's strength.

Media "Market" Mistakes

Example 1: Intel announced (08.19.10) its $7.68B acquisition of McAfee, a leading purveyor of security software. The *Wall Street Journal* reported this acquisition as follows:

> *Intel, based near McAfee in Santa Clara, CA, supplies more than 80% of the microprocessors that serve as calculating engines in PCs and server systems. Though that business is healthy right now, the company has long acknowledged that, without diversifying, it can't grow any faster than that* **market**.

Mistake: The last sentence: "... can't grow any faster than that market." There's *no* market, only an industry segment, a product category. Products (PCs and server systems) are *not* markets.

Example 2: Dell announced, on September 2, 2010, its exit from the bidding war with HP over data-storage vendor 3PAR. TradingMarkets.com's reportage included this bit:

> *The public bidding war between HP and Dell came as the two personal computer giants are striving to diversify their business and push into enterprise data center as well as other more profitable **markets**.*

Mistake: See that last word, markets? Wrong! Proper term is industry or product segment. Am I nitpicking? Tell a CPA that assets and liabilities are synonymous.

Example 3: On March 2, 2011, Apple announced its iPad 2. TechCrunch's reportage included this sentence:

> *After selling 15 million iPads in 2010 and gaining 90% market share in the tablet **market**, Apple is ready to take the next step.*

Mistake: There's *no* such thing as a tablet market. The correct term is tablet industry, business, or product segment. Am I neurotic? Tell a physicist that a proton and electron are synonymous.

Example 4: The *Wall Street Journal* reported (05.10.11) that Microsoft purchased Skype for $8.5B. Its reportage included this sentence:

> *Skype could play a role in Microsoft's effort to turn around its fortunes in the mobile-phone **market**, an area where it has lagged badly behind rivals Apple and Google.*

Mistake: There's *no* mobile-phone "market." Industry, business, or product segment would be the correct term. A product is a market as an artery is a vein.

Example 5: On August 18, 2011, FoxNews.com reported that HP will jettison its tablet, smartphone, and PC divisions. This article is chock-full of market malaprops:

> ... *high-end server and software* ***markets****, worldwide computer market, 12.9% of the worldwide* ***market****, 10.7% of the* ***market****.*

Mistake: The three market mentions above are incorrect. There's *no* software market. Only one proper use of market in this piece: "The move echoes one from IBM, HP's rival for the enterprise market [correctly meaning customers], which, in 2005, sold off its computer business to Lenovo, the biggest maker of PCs in China."

Example 6: On August 8, 2013, *Wall Street Journal* reported "Android Keeps Obliterating Smartphone **Market**."

> *While Google's Android operating system continues to distance itself from the competition in the worldwide smartphone* ***market****, one-time* ***market*** *leader BlackBerry is reaching new lows.*

Mistake: There is *no* smartphone market; there is a smartphone industry. There is *no* market leader; there is an *industry* leader.

Example 7: On August 23, 2013, *USA Today* reported that Microsoft CEO Steve Ballmer will retire within 12 months. In the first sentence of the article, we read:

> *Microsoft says Steve Ballmer will retire as the company's CEO within 12 months, as the tech giant navigates a rapidly changing computer **market**.*

Mistake: There's *no* computer market and certainly no "rapidly changing" computer market. There is, *as I've stated ad nauseam,* a computer industry.

Why do I keep harping on this? Because in no other discipline or profession is terminology-swapping tolerated. Not in finance, physics, medicine, or engineering. On 10.03.12, Dominique Turpin, president of IMD, a Swiss business school, made this accurate observation in a *Forbes* magazine article entitled "The CMO Is Dead":

> *"Nobody has a clear idea of what marketing is. It's fuzzy. Ask 20 senior managers in any company what marketing is, and they will give 20 different answers. By contrast, most people would agree on a definition of finance or production."*

Respect Marketing Terminology

If anyone in a hospital's vascular-surgery department would dare utter "incompetent *arterial* valves," he would be ridiculed and scolded, and likely fired—unless, of course, he works for a union or the government. Why? Only *veins* have valves. Arteries don't have valves. Swapping artery and vein is unheard of. Can you imagine 20 doctors giving 20 different answers to the question, What is a vein? You can't. If medical professionals don't respect and correctly use proper medical terminology, their profession will wither and patients will die.

Likewise, CEOs and their marketers will keep failing if they don't respect and correctly use marketing terms. Alas, "market" has become the commerce equivalent of doohickey, a generic catch-all word for the vocabulary-challenged.

When CEOs and their staffs misuse *market*, no people will die, but brands will suffer. This establishes a self-fulfilling dismissal of marketing and branding as superfluous, money-wasting activities to cut in economic downturns.

Your Product Is Mute

Engineers and lawyers are polar opposites: the former being reliably black-and-white, the latter annoyingly gray (Bill Clinton: "It depends upon what the meaning of the word 'is' is").

Yet, there's a parallel, or so it seems: the negligence case with no direct witnesses, where circumstantial evidence is the sole weapon. In such a case, the plaintiff's counsel (PC) will argue *res ipsa loquitur*: the thing speaks for itself. But, despite the "res" argument, judge and jury don't instantly accede: the PC *must* make the case; this can take days, weeks, or months. The thing speaks for itself? It seems not.

Judging by the sea of generic, jargonized homepages, brochures, ads, speeches, and sales pitches—which resemble data sheets, nutritional labels, and catalogs—the scribes of such pablum clearly believe: "the product speaks for itself; if prospects can't hear it, they'll have to listen better."

In fact, *your product does not speak for itself.* Frankly, nothing speaks for itself; otherwise, you'd win every argument simply by presenting the facts. Our replacement Latin phrase is res ipsa *non* loquitur, or the thing does *not* speak for itself. Great trial lawyers and marketers already know this.

Your product is mute; *you* must give it a voice, the voice of the customer—*not* your voice, *not* the voice of your company, technology, or industry. The voice of the customer is the *only* one he can hear. We seldom get this voice. Why?

Most folks can't communicate, in any form (ask their spouses); yet, they're the ones creating and controlling their companies' brands. Attend any pitch event in Silicon Valley, a forum where aspiring entrepreneurs convey their business ideas to a gaggle of investors, hoping to raise equity capital.

Sequentially, each wannabe titan presents his plan for a better mobile/social mousetrap, in arcane mousetrapese, predictably unable to specify why anyone would *need* and buy his mousetrap. He craves his comfort zone, believing that:

- His product speaks for itself (it speaks to him)
- He need only preach to his choir (his clones)
- Customer language breaches the techie creed.

Following this agonizing exercise, mystified investors, in succession, laboriously attempt to grasp each company's raison d'être. No matter the event or roster of entrepreneurs, the aforementioned dynamics are identical.

Invariably, when I ask why he founded his company, the typical entrepreneur answers: *Mobile is what's in now; it's what interests the VCs* [venture capitalists]. No mention of real customer needs or problems to solve—just a me-too, product-focused mentality. Again, I call this *technologica erotica*.

Fortunately, on rare occasions, a vendor succeeds with brilliant branding. Below is an ad from Gillette for its Mach3 razor. It features the voice of the customer—*how much she wants to kiss him*—not product features. If you think this example doesn't apply to industrial and commercial domains, think again. Without GutShare, there's no branding.

CHAPTER FIVE

Branding vs. Marketing

Most people don't understand the true definitions of market, marketing, and branding (see Chapters 1-3); so, how can any company message itself properly? Bingo. It's rare.

Branding is the arrowhead of marketing. Marketing is the discipline of the four P's: product, price, placement, and promotion. Marketers are responsible for identifying and analyzing the characteristics, habits, habitats, needs, and desires of future and current customers—then formulating, delivering, and branding the resultant products (and services) accordingly.

In his 2011 biography, *Steve Jobs*, Walter Isaacson related a quote from Mr. Jobs about market research:

> *"Some people say, 'Give the customers what they want.' But that's not my approach. Our job is to figure out what they're going to want before they do. I think Henry Ford once said, 'If I'd asked customers what they wanted, they would have told me, "A faster horse!"' People don't know what they want until you show it to them. That's why I never rely on market research. Our task is to read things that are not yet on the page."*

I mean no disrespect to the late Mr. Jobs, but his dismissal of market (customer) research is disingenuous. He said his job was to *figure out* what people wanted before they did, to *read* things that are not yet on the page. How did Jobs do all that "figuring out" and "reading things"?

He did it by knowing Apple's prospective and actual customers in great detail; he was better at it than everyone. Mr. Jobs was a master of market (customer) research!

It's true that people don't know what *solutions* they'll buy—they have no idea what's possible—but they *do* know their needs and wishes. They *do* know what problems they must solve, before any vendors show them solutions; they just don't know in what forms, and at what costs, these solutions will appear.

When I consult for companies, I ask their customers about success-inhibitors, *not "imagined" solutions*. I have the skill to draw them out, to get them to talk about themselves and their challenges, Market research can be formal and informal. I typically use written surveys, Internet polls, and face-to-face interviews—whatever will yield the data I need.

*Customers cannot and don't envision new products; vendors **never** should ask them to do so*. Customers love to talk about *themselves* all day long; they don't want to talk about vendors.

To create a tagline for a restaurant, I walked around asking patrons, eating at tables and drinking at the bar, *why* they liked the bistro and *why* they frequented the place. This methodology was exactly what the situation warranted, and it yielded what I needed to wordsmith the tagline. The client was happy and still uses my tagline. So, why couldn't the client do this solo? *Because the client lacked the skills and knew it.*

Recently, I caught a rerun of the iconic 1987 hit *Wall Street*, starring Michael Douglas and Charlie Sheen. Always one to glean a fresh insight with every repeat of a great movie, I found in this screening a branding gem.

Bud Fox (Sheen), a trader in a brokerage house, had tried but failed for 59 consecutive days to meet personally with Gordon Gekko (Douglas), the master investment banker. But, on Gekko's birthday, Fox prevailed, Cuban cigars in tow.

After exchanging a few awkward pleasantries about the young trader's admirable persistence, Gekko gave Fox an immutable lesson in Branding 101 by asking him, *"Why am I listening to you?"*

Bingo. Why should *any* prospect listen to a vendor? Inherent in Gekko's fundamental question was this kernel: *What do you know about me?* Aha! The only way Fox could glean anything about Gekko was through, you guessed it, market research.

Gekko didn't ask about Fox's company or products. As the prospect, he wanted to talk only about *himself* and his needs: specifically, illegal insider information. Once Bud Fox grasped and then addressed Gordon Gekko's needs, he got his attention—and his cash. No kidding.

Dale Carnegie, in his *How to Win Friends and Influence People,* taught us*:* Talk to people about *themselves*, in *their* language; they'll listen for hours. Branding 101. So, why does your company continue to talk to *itself* with arcane jargon?

If you unwisely ask future and current customers to envision your new products (your language), you'll fail at market research and, consequently, at branding. Henry Ford knew that his potential buyers wanted "faster horses"—their only benchmark. But, he keenly perceived their **real** desire: *to reach their destinations faster and more conveniently.* Result: the Model T was born; it was a whopping success.

The Marketing-Branding Divide

OK. You've done your market (customer) research. You've identified a specific target market (group of relevant prospects). You've formulated, priced, created, and tested a product that will solve customers' problems or grant their wishes. You've chosen the sales channels. Now, you have to articulate its value to customers, investors, analysts, and reporters. What do you say and write?

Congratulations. You've just crossed the marketing-branding divide. *What do you say and write?* Alas, the art of wordsmithing the corporate or any product's customer-centric value proposition—*branding*—is absent in your company. The ability to make a concise, unique pitch that is evocative, memorable, and repeatable resides in no employee, PR firm, or ad agency. Because of your company's past jargonizing, conventional thinking, and misconceptions, however, you may be unaware of that.

Your immediate reflex is to crank up that old jargon generator: *We sell the fastest, smallest, cheapest, most state-of-the-art widget in the world.* **Caution:** You've demoted your product to commodity status, with a pitch that is identical to the white noise your competitors spew; it excites nobody.

How many times have we seen brilliant, accomplished, capable people in front of lecterns or TV cameras ramble on and on about something or other, boring us silly? There's no difference between a CEO and product lacking a strong, concise, unique, memorable message. Just because one is skilled in the four P's of *marketing* does not make him skilled in *branding.* Not even close. Not even remotely close.

So what? Should you care that your branding sucks? Should you care if neither your employees nor your customers nor investors nor reporters nor analysts can articulate your brand—*without mentioning your product?* Does it matter that your homepage is a naked homage to products and engineers, that it resembles a cockpit's dials, gauges, and switches—and is so impossible to grasp and navigate that your salespeople and customers ignore it?

After all, you *are* ringing up sales, notwithstanding your murky homepage; that's what counts, right? You rely on your costly direct and indirect channels to close deals. So, to hell with all that branding bullshit.

Question: Why do manufacturers of cars, yachts, jets, trains, and other vehicles constantly embed lighter, stronger materials into their products? Is it not for increased speed at lower operating cost? And, by doing this, wouldn't the vendors make themselves more appealing and competitive?

A strong brand is akin to the sleeker, lighter jet: it gets your value proposition to its target destinations—customers, investors, analysts, and reporters—faster and cheaper.

Alternatively, you can tolerate a weak brand—a heavy, slow, gas-guzzling tank—and rely instead on your expensive, hard-to-manage salesforce. Worse, you can hope and pray that customers randomly or inadvertently stumble upon your company, and then purchase your products.

I was the founding VP of marketing at a startup. The CEO/founder, an MIT geek, met alone with an angel investor to seek a $250K infusion. It was supposed to be a slam-dunk, but he didn't write that check. Why? The CEO didn't know. Really. So, I got a meeting alone with this angel, a computer-industry luminary, in his kitchen. I presented our company and product so simply that a 3rd-grader could grasp them. **Result:** this PhD got it right away and was in for $250K. Did I possess the detailed product knowledge of the founder? Not even close. Still, I knew how to articulate its value proposition, which I had created, and do so compellingly. Brand matters.

Never forget: marketing without a strong brand is like shooting an arrow without an arrowhead.

CHAPTER SIX

Politics of Branding

When someone opines on a matter, sans supporting facts and expertise, her opinion is invalid. Yet, she, and her ilk, will vote for the best-sounding bloviator in the political field, because facts matter little to her—and to the bloviating politician. We then see this narcissist, who affects our rights and wealth, fighting his rivals over laws that will destroy us— not for *our* good but for the prestige of *personal* victory.

So, we learn, to our consternation, that those holding invalid opinions, who are asked nonetheless to submit those opinions, ultimately wield a lot of power. This phenomenon also occurs in business, especially in branding, which, it so happens, is extremely political.

In no company would a CEO ask marketers to write software code or legal briefs, or balance the books, nor would he seek their opinions on such matters—they lack expertise. Yet, in nearly every company, the CEO allows and encourages employees, from myriad backgrounds, sans expertise, to opine on and participate in branding strategies and tactics.

As I've indicated, there's a pervasive presumption in organizations of all kinds that marketing requires no special knowledge and skills, and that anyone who can spell "social media" qualifies for the job. Result: branding by committee.

When so-called leaders lack understanding of topics, when they want to avoid making tough decisions, and when they want people to view them as politically correct, they form committees and taskforces. A committee's dynamic is always political, its output always uninspiring, unmemorable, and unrepeatable pablum. I've lived it. I've observed it.

To wit: from the *homepage* of IBM, the world's second-largest software company. One wonders how many branding-committee signatures were required to approve this inexplicable message: *Smarter Computing. What's Next. Ready Now. See how new cloud and data-centric solutions help you achieve a software-defined environment.* Huh?

Occasionally, we encounter a clueless branding tyrant, who intimidates those who know better into rubber-stamping his or her ideas. In one of my consulting gigs, a clueless but powerful board member forced her wrongheaded branding opinions onto the company, causing it to make huge mistakes and almost sink. My presence enabled the others to fight back, but this internecine war was a costly distraction for the young startup. She should have deferred to the experts.

Fortune magazine, in the 05.21.12 issue, featured "How HP Lost Its Way." Read this eye-popping excerpt about a disastrous former CEO, Léo Apotheker (he lasted 10 months), who forced an idiotic, widely panned tagline on HP:

> *Consider Apotheker's attempt, earlier that year, to find a catchy phrase that could define HP. He settled on a head-scratcher: "Everybody on." Instead of opposing the idea, almost every executive told Apotheker it was a great slogan (with at least one whispering behind his back that it was horrible). Only Joshi was willing to speak up. "I don't get this," he told Apotheker when the slogan was unveiled at a meeting. Joshi earned the CEO's wrath. The campaign launched—and promptly bombed. As one tech blog headline described the debut, HP'S "EVERYBODY ON" AD GOES TO THE GRAMMYS, CAUSES NATIONWIDE CRINGING.*

I could have filled this entire book with stories like the Apotheker saga. Unfortunately, invalid opinions often rule; it is difficult, and often suicidal, for the competent ones to dare overturn them—even branding warriors want their paychecks!

Here's another beauty, from years ago, courtesy of the Cisco Systems branding committee. *Can we please stop the Kumbaya talk of bringing the world closer together?* At some point, *somebody* has to lead. Question: If everyone is "working together," which never has happened and never will happen—anywhere in the world—who makes the freaking decisions? Cisco's unfathomable campaign bombed, of course:

There's no way—no way—that skilled branding pros, *with clout*, would create, approve, and display such nebulous white noise. Why does it appear and reappear? Amateurs rule.

In 2012, Kraft Foods split into two public companies: a food & beverage company, Kraft Foods Group (Velveeta, Kool-Aid, Maxwell House), and a snack-food company, Mondelēz International (Cadbury, Trident, Ritz). The Mondelēz moniker was the result of a five-month "co-creation" process of 1000+ employees (*a megacommittee*), who, according to *Business Week*, submitted 1700 names. Two men, an IT guy in Vienna and the company's general counsel, neither of whom has any branding chops, created this *CEO-approved* "winner"; their weird concoction, which means "delicious world," proves it.

Can you imagine Mondelēz, or any company, staging a companywide competition for the best way to sue a copyright or patent infringer? Oh, I forgot: lawyering requires special skills—branding doesn't.

Horse or Camel?

We're constantly bombarded with billboards, print ads, commercials, and homepages that convey no or negative value and are, simply, colossal branding failures. There's no doubt in my mind that committees generate this junk. Few branding efforts fare worse than those of GEICO, the insurance carrier, with its rotating cast of weird characters and inconsistent messages. We've seen the green lizard and now get the camel.

Branding, like gourmet cooking, requires specific and special expertise, singular talent, and unique flair. Assigning this endeavor to a team of generalists, geeks, investors, inept communicators, lawyers, and HQ-bound ivory-tower-dwellers will result in failure. Committees, always political, produce bland, banal, baffling messaging—squandering time, money, and competitive advantages. *Too many chefs spoil the broth.*

In addition to Mark Wahlberg and Charlize Theron, the Mini Cooper was a real star of *The Italian Job.* British Motor Corporation launched the first Mini in 1957, based on simple specifications that Sir Alec Issigonis and his team of eight used in their iconic design. Issigonis epitomized "less is more" and gave us this memorable gem: *A camel is a horse designed by committee.* Indeed.

Anyone who's been on *any* committee knows how mindnumbingly unproductive, uncreative, and political it can be. Typically, a "leader" who will not or cannot lead creates committees and councils to avoid making decisions, to kick the can down the road.

Branding—the art of articulating a unique, compelling, memorable, repeatable value proposition—requires decisive leadership, the guts to stand apart from the competition. This is *not* a job for a committee. A committee excels at converting clarity into ambiguity. Politicians excel at ambiguity.

I've observed many companies, in both my consulting and executive experiences, especially in today's "we-must feel-good-about-ourselves" culture, exulting in squishy, politically correct, all-opinions-count branding by committee. As I've posited before, committees don't work. Committees are about nebulous consensus, not boldness and creativity. Committees are illusions for action; they create white noise—not unique, sharp arrowheads.

Barack Obama loves committees. Do you remember his National Commission on Fiscal Responsibility and Reform of 2010, headed by Alan Simpson and Erskine Bowles? This body made strong, actionable recommendations, which Mr. Obama promptly ignored. Since then, the deficit and debt have skyrocketed.

Let's not forget Obama's President's Council on Jobs and Competitiveness, which he created in 2009. Its chairman is Jeffrey Immelt, CEO of GE, whose stock has declined by half during his 12 years at the helm. *Form a council to create jobs? Since when do councils create jobs?* Try cutting the Politburo-style taxes, spending, entitlements, and regulations. During a meeting of this feckless council, Obama joked that "shovel-ready was not as shovel-ready as we expected." The joke's on us. Our GDP is growing at an annualized 1.7%. We have a whopping 15% *real* unemployment rate, 91M are out of the labor force, and 48M are on foodstamps. Committees ruin economies, too.

Committees, lacking incentive, expertise, and desire to win, ruin brands. Committees are merely illusions for action; they exist to help make the insecure feel needed. Committees are clouds, not arrowheads, and have no place in branding.

By the same token, letting an out-of-his-depth tyrant run branding is equally a formula for failure. When people are afraid to, or structurally cannot, challenge that tyrant, bad decisions emerge. FDR decided the price of gold from his bed, thereby injuring the economy. LBJ chose bombing targets in

Vietnam, thereby injuring American soldiers. Léo Apotheker picked a stupid tagline, injuring HP's brand.

Before initiating your branding effort—which you must do *before* building a product—make a pivotal decision: horse or camel, memorable epicurean event or potluck supper. Let the true branding experts run branding, and then make sure they're getting results. And, remove politics from branding.

CHAPTER SEVEN
Fear of Branding

Throughout this book, in numerous places, I cite and illustrate the fear of branding. It's real, so significant that it deserves a special chapter. Why? *People do more to avoid pain than to seek pleasure.* This truth influences the behaviors and deliverables of your branding staff, whom you hire.

What is the pain of branding? What about branding do people fear? **Standing out, naked and exposed**. They fear ridicule from challenging convention and being unique—inside and outside their companies. They fear failure as a result of being unique. They fear professional ostracism.

After Senator Ted Cruz staged a 21-hour filibuster to defund Obamacare, his wimpy brethren chastised him: *You obviously don't know how Washington works.* Said Chris Matthews, MSNBC's chief Obamaphile: "I think Ted Cruz is brilliant. The president has met his match in this guy."

Often, I hear the following refrain from my clients after creating for them messaging that's unique, bold, provocative, memorable, and repeatable: *Well, nobody else is doing that.* No shit. Welcome to Uniqueville!

Do you remember when Steve Jobs created the "Think Different" campaign, in 1997, to save Apple from bankruptcy? It was revolutionary. It was brilliant. Everybody talked about it. Duh! Steve's message was simple: *Apple is unique. No company is like Apple, we're unafraid to say so, and don't you forget it!* It worked. Jobs never worried about standing out. People admire and gravitate to those who have the balls to stand out, to be unique.

Fox News star Bill O'Reilly recently published *Killing Jesus*, after enjoying enormous success with his previous history tomes, *Killing Lincoln* and *Killing Kennedy*. O'Reilly sat for an interview with Norah O'Donnell of *60 Minutes* to discuss his book. Among her many questions: "The title 'Killing,' a bit sensationalist?" O'Reilly's rejoinder: "Of course. Of course it's sensationalist. That's who I am. I'm a sensationalist. I'm a big mouth. I get attention. In this world, if you want a mass-market presentation, you have to get attention." Bingo.

Bill O'Reilly knows that he can't get attention by copying his competitors and blending in. His two-word book titles are brilliant: unique, concise, compelling, memorable, and repeatable. See a pattern here? He's been #1 in cable news for 13 years. It's not luck or accidental.

Ironically, Lexus has been promoting its 2014 IS sport sedan on TV with unique spots advocating to target buyers that *it's more exciting to blend out than blend in.* It's true, but, for many, blending out is *un*exciting—it's mortifying. Clearly, Lexus is *not* trying to appeal to the masses.

Let me clarify a point about the masses, vis-à-vis the strategies of Bill O'Reilly and Lexus: The masses are *attracted* to singular people and companies, but few within the masses want to, or can, *be* singular. And, *that* is why so few people are suitable for branding. Remember that when hiring them.

Discomfort Zone

Branding requires being a unique standout from the white noise of me-too competition. Standing out, or blending out, as Lexus states it, to most people, is painful; they fear it. People like to blend in. They crave the comfort of fraternity and conformity—perfect for a coffee klatch but terrible for a branding team.

If you fear expressing your opinion in a group setting, say a cocktail party, because it runs counter to the prevailing view in the room, and you fear retaliation—being labeled an outcast or being shunned—you are *not* branding material. OK, but you're the CEO. So what?

As a "blender" CEO, you're likely to veto a brilliant branding idea because it isn't *your* style, not something *you* would create—and it makes *you* uncomfortable. Your veto could cost your company millions in lost opportunities. Here's a better idea: *veto your discomfort!*

How does fear of branding manifest in your company? People inhabit one of three zones: comfort, indecision, and discomfort. In the figure below, we see that the *comfort zone,*

AKA Jargonville, is where the blenders live. It is the smallest of the three zones, because people have small comfort zones.

The next zone is for *indecision*. Notice that people, to feel "safe," vacillate between comfort and indecision. When push comes to shove, they'll revert to comfort. They love that nobody-will-fire-me-for-using-jargon feeling.

Finally, we arrive at the *discomfort zone*, Uniqueville, where *real* branders live. It's the largest because most people have lots of fears and avoid treading here. Hire those who don't fear this zone; *listen to them, even if they're not like you.*

CHAPTER EIGHT

Word of Mouth

I met with the founding partner of an up-and-coming law firm to discuss branding. "Isn't success really all about word of mouth?" he asked. "Yes, but **which** word?" I replied.

I continued: "If you don't supply and manage the word you want your clients to spread, they'll use the words *they* choose." In fact, it was already happening.

Word of mouth, or buzz, is the "message" we broadcast to others after reacting *emotionally* to products, companies, people, experiences, books, articles, opinions, speeches, and performances. The question is, *Which* words do we broadcast?

Failure to articulate uniquely, compellingly, succinctly, and memorably your value proposition—*in customer language, not industry jargon, not product vernacular*—is failure to manage your brand, your buzz, your word of mouth. You'll create a branding vacuum. And, because nature abhors a vacuum, others—employees, customers, investors, analysts, channel/alliance partners, and reporters—will fill it, for sure. This is a preventable management disaster.

Manage Your Word of Mouth

Investors Employees

Reporters Analysts

Partners Customers

Or, They'll Manage It for You!

© 2014 MarcRudov.com

Next time you're at a party, ask the guests to describe a Chevy Malibu. You'll see puzzled looks. Then, ask them to portray a Corvette. Without even thinking, they'll be detailing its iconic stingray design. Two Chevy brands, one unique.

Unique is binary: it either exists or it doesn't (no such thing as "fairly" unique). Few brands are unique, fewer remain unique: in most cases, a unique brand quickly gets demoted to distinctive or, worse, ordinary, as competitors copy it.

Unfortunately, too many vendors fall in love with their brands, believing they're unique and self-explanatory. Such insular thinking begets cloudy, arcane messaging—and the assumption that customers will grasp their products as easily and enthusiastically as the designers who created them.

I spoke with a CEO at a healthcare startup, pointing out his homepage's murkiness. He confirmed my critique by admitting that viewers *just don't grasp it.* When I pointed out that his homepage lacked a unique, crystal-clear, memorable value proposition, he balked and blamed—to my surprise—a weak user interface. By that statement, he meant inadequate technology. In fact, his weak user interface was the absence of compelling language, but he didn't want to admit it. He'll let his company remain unfathomable, continuing to allow others to define it (as a confusing mess) with words *they* choose to spread, if they bother at all. This is a common error.

After joining a Fortune 1000 firm as a top marketing exec, I discovered total chaos. Each country manager was branding us differently to his customer base, according to *his* perception of our brand—no direction from HQ. This branding vacuum left our country managers no choice. With sales quotas to meet, they used words they hoped would work; I didn't blame them. After I supplied them unified branding that worked worldwide, they enthusiastically embraced it and successfully leveraged it. Word of mouth began to spread, internally and externally, for the first time in many years.

Also, upon my arrival, I found our PR folks issuing seven-page news releases—*and getting no ink.* No word of mouth. I immediately instituted a new rule: no news release to exceed two pages; every product mention within the release must contain customer value/benefits. Within weeks, we were getting ink. I visited the trade editors, who told me that, prior to my tenure, they never had understood our messaging—and, therefore, weren't motivated to write about us. Duh!

Every company needs positive, strong word of mouth—*it's much cheaper than advertising*. Like a budget, the CEO must manage word of mouth—or it will manage her. Nature is always ready, willing, and able to fill a branding vacuum.

Letting others define your company is the antithesis of branding, a blunder that you, the CEO, never should tolerate: it needlessly raises your costs of sales, capital, and media. In the word-vs.-mouth battle, *word must win*. It's message over megaphone. Never use a megaphone without a message.

In a heated political campaign, the weaker candidate's opponent(s), and the media, will define him. Mitt Romney, a strong executive but a weak campaigner, experienced this. Alas, Romney was unable to fill this branding vacuum. To win voters, a candidate must define himself, as a company must define itself to win customers.

Neurosurgery Is Complicated

On 10.02.13, Bill O'Reilly of Fox News Channel interviewed Dr. Ben Carson, professor emeritus of pediatric neurosurgery at Johns Hopkins University School of Medicine, about the unfathomable Obamacare:

O'Reilly: *"Nobody understands this law. I mean, I've tried and tried and tried. Give me your take on Obamacare."*

Carson: *"What I would always tell the residents, before I retired, is, 'Neurosurgery is complicated, and you're dealing with people [patients] who haven't been trained in neurosurgery, but if you cannot explain it to them in a way that they understand, then you shouldn't be operating on them.' And, by the same token, we shouldn't be rolling out a program that most people have no idea about. I don't think even the people who proposed it understand it, quite frankly."*

It matters not how "cool" your product is: If you can't explain it, succinctly, you can't sell it. When your product is complicated, like neurosurgery, this situation is compounded. If you don't simplify it, *in customer language*, you're in trouble.

Those who hear your arcane presentation or pitch will comprehend *some* of your words, interpret those words according to their abilities, convert your words into *their* words, and, *maybe*, spread their words. Most likely, if people don't understand your words, they'll forget you within a few minutes and go back to whatever they were doing. This is a branding disaster that too many companies repeat.

Surely you remember that childhood game, radio. All the kids sit in a circle. The teacher whispers a word in one kid's ear; he then whispers it into the next kid's ear, and so on around the circle to the last kid. What always happens? The last kid and first kid compare words, and discover that they have *different words.* Why? Because people communicate *what they think they hear.* The difference is, our childhood game uses just one word! Now, imagine what people interpret from the generic jargon on your homepage!

Customers, investors, analysts, and reporters always feel better about your product—and therefore will "spread the word" about it—when they can explain it to others, *in your absence.* Doesn't this make sense, inherently?

When using the "right" word—conveyed in a unique, succinct, compelling, memorable, repeatable way—the mouth spreading it is irrelevant. That way, all your employees and contractors and alliance partners can stay on-message.

Conversely, when employing the wrong word—*generic, boring, forgettable, unrepeatable jargon*—the mouth spreading it is paramount. Such a practice, unfortunately the rule in most of Corporate America, requires a specific, expensive, skilled, usually unavailable mouth to explain the company or product. This is a costly, ineffective practice. Remember: without powerful word of mouth—buzz—there is no brand.

So, to answer the question I posed above, *Which* word of mouth? It's up to *you.*

CHAPTER NINE
Branding & Sales

Perhaps you're tired of hearing this from me, but I'm not stopping: Most homepages are utterly ineffective and offputting. They read like nutrition labels, newspapers, and catalogues. They're sales-killers.

As potential buyers, we want to see on your homepage that you understand *us*. What do we see instead? Lots about your products—with the implicit assumption that we land on your homepage, knowing we want to buy your product, credit card in hand. Hubris of the highest order. Why should we give a crap about you? We don't.

In 2008, I wrote about Hewlett-Packard's site and will repeat the gist of my observations and conclusions here—because they're timeless and illustrative; besides, little has changed about it since then, when Mark Hurd was CEO. The premise of my article was that the Website, a company's most-ubiquitous billboard, is its sole external face if its salesforce quits tomorrow. Alas, this is the typical implied message from most corporate sites: *We don't know what you need. So, we'll talk to ourselves. We love our products; can you tell?*

When arriving at HP's site, the first thing shoved in my face was a printer. Was I at Office Depot or Staples? HP's site was (is), essentially, a product catalog. Now, what value would the CIO of a major corporation, with no HP experience other than buying its printers, get out of visiting this site? Little. It says nothing about HP's value proposition (brand) and why he'll benefit from visiting there.

Given that HP had just delivered an impressive Q208 ($28.3B in net revenues; 9% GAAP operating profit of $2.6B), the company was clearly doing well—in spite of its site. So, why even bother having one?

HP's imaging and printer group contributed 27% of the revenues and about 40% of the operating profits in Q208. Is that why it's hawking printers so aggressively? I don't think so. I think the site just isn't given high priority, despite being a major branding vehicle.

My cursory read of the situation was that HP's direct channels (salesforce and consultants) and indirect channels (retail chains, systems integrators) were primarily responsible for communicating HP's brand to prospects and customers. That is a universal mistake, which raises the cost of sales.

To demonstrate what HP *could have conveyed* on its homepage, let's examine some excerpts from its 2007 annual report:

- *Three factors contributed to HP's growth: the explosion of digital information and content; the growing need for technology that enables people* to create, store, share, and print that content; and the rapidly growing demand for information technology (IT) in emerging markets around the world.

- Feeding the worldwide demand for information and rich digital content is the enormous expansion of search engines, blogs, social networks, e-mail, text messages, and online video and images.

- To complicate matters, this content often lacks authentication and proper security, and it is increasingly global and mobile. Potentially hundreds of millions of new users in emerging markets are coming online—from small-business owners in China to farmers in Brazil to consumers in Eastern Europe.

- At the same time, the expectations of consumers have changed. People want instantaneous access to content. They expect this accessibility regardless of what kind of device they are using or where they happen to be. And their tolerance for complexity is low.

- Dealing with all this data—and rising consumer expectations—is a huge and disruptive challenge for our customers and their IT environments and a major opportunity for HP. It puts pressure on businesses to rebuild, retool, *and deploy a flexible infrastructure so they can get the right information to the right people at the right time.*

- *Customers will need systems, software, and services to create, store, and analyze content; PCs and handheld devices to access and share it; and monitors, TVs, and printers to view and print it. Many companies can do some of these things, but we believe that HP is the only company with the portfolio and partnerships to do them all.*

Key Points from These Paragraphs:

- People want instantaneous access to content. They expect this accessibility regardless of what kind of device they are using or where they happen to be. **And their tolerance for complexity is low**.
- It puts pressure on businesses to rebuild, retool, and deploy a flexible infrastructure so they can **get the right information to the right people at the right time**.
- Many companies can do some of these things, but we believe that **HP is the only company with the portfolio and partnerships to do them all**.

I saw *none* of these salient statements, in any form, on HP's homepage, *whose complexity was high.* Yet, HP marketers could have wordsmithed them easily and powerfully into a compelling value proposition (brand) that unequivocally and uniquely answers the simple question: *Why HP?*

What would happen if *your* salesforce quits tomorrow, leaving your Website as the *only* means of communicating with, and selling products to, the outside world. Now, take a good look at your Website. Are you willing to stake your job on it?

Selling Kills Sales

Words—love, hate, lawsuit, bailout, bankruptcy—elicit strong emotions and behaviors in and from us. Selling is no exception: it leads to defensiveness, where a purchaser feels that an unneeded or unwanted product will be pushed on him. This dynamic is both a mood killer and a sales killer.

There often is a huge disconnect between vendor and customer—originating with words. As I illustrated in the third chapter, your product is not a market. Vendors falsely equate markets with products. Wireless market? No such thing. Markets contain purchasers, not products. Misusing these words, consequently, causes branding dissonance.

By the same token, the words "selling" and "sales" cause branding disconnect and dissonance. Any user of these words tends to focus inward—on the vendor-centric agenda: product, quota, bonus, commission, output, inventory, profit, and stock price.

Guess what? Purchasers don't think or care about your vendor-centric agenda. They have an agenda to acquire value—employing metrics like ROI, security, cost of ownership, and ease of use. Therein lies the conflict: one party is selling, the other seeking value.

Early in my career, each boss told me to construct a unique selling proposition, or USP, a simple phrase designed to capture the essence of our product. This was wrong, and I didn't realize it until years later. Notice how many USPs—*We run the tightest ship in the shipping business* (an old USP of United Parcel Service)—are product/company-centric, devoid of the customer. Now, UPS uses *We Love Logistics*, which is more appealing to customers' supply-chain pains.

A few years back, I was consulting for a producer of trader turrets used on the massive trading floors of investment banks. I visited several of my client's customers on Wall Street and asked each (typically a VP of trading administration) to articulate the biggest problem he faced every day—not necessarily related to technology or my client's product. **Surprise:** *No one had ever asked such a question!* Why? Vendors tend to focus on products and selling.

The complaint: my client's salespeople were constantly bypassing these decisionmakers and selling directly to "star" traders. Back in the heyday of Wall Street, star traders were untouchable and incorrigible, wreaking budgetary havoc on their employers, and my client was totally unaware of it. Why? Focused on selling, focused on products.

Because, for the first time, I had brought back *new* information about nonproduct problems, my client resolved the issue and increased customer satisfaction. *Focus on value increases sales.*

Customers seek value, not products. As the CEO, therefore, you must become a *value* executive, not a sales executive. And, by the way, customers know the difference.

As long as your company exhibits a palpable "selling" orientation, while your customers have a value agenda, the result will be branding disconnect and dissonance. This is how selling kills your sales.

I'm not suggesting that you eliminate your salesforce— an absurd move—just all evidence of a selling *orientation*. Replace your unique selling proposition with a unique *value* proposition, and your customers will respond accordingly—as will your sales.

Use Mirrors to Attract Customers

Window shopping is the practice of viewing, but not purchasing, the merchandise displayed in a storefront. Such ephemeral browsing is not limited to storefronts. It also occurs on homepages, magazine ads, billboards, and TV commercials. Why? Lack of connection.

People make purchases when, with easy convincing, they believe those purchases will solve their problems or grant their wishes. They do not want to, nor should they, exert any energy to figure out a vendor's product. This is the vendor's total responsibility.

How does this work? The vendor/brander creates messaging that reflects customers' needs right back in their faces. Sales 101. The best branding vehicle is, therefore, a mirror.

Unfortunately, the branding vehicle used most often is a window. Take the typical homepage, for example. It is a window fronting a product display. The prospect who happens upon this window views the merchandise—elaborately arrayed and labeled—and asks a fundamental question: *What about me?* Indeed.

I can't repeat this axiom enough times, even if you're tired of hearing it: People buy product value and benefits, *not products*. Unless vendors brand their products in customer language, there are no product benefits and, consequently, nothing to buy.

And, falling back on that worn and tired claim, "saves time and money," is not branding. It is not a unique value proposition. It is boring, lazy, unimaginative, overused white-noise drivel.

Donald Trump knows this axiom quite well. He sells opulence and prestige, *not real estate*, and makes that quite clear with his messaging mirror. Wealthy people around the world respond well to what they see in Trump's mirror.

Before purchasing any vendor's products—whether consumer, commercial, or military—customers try to imagine themselves using, sharing, and benefiting from them. If they can't conjure any gut reactions, window shopping is the likely result.

In any branding campaign, the customer—not your product—must be the star. And, the customer must feel that he's the star and will remain so after owning your product. Look at your homepage. Is your customer the star?

Displaying products and reciting their attributes will not convince anyone to become a customer. Unless the prospect's plight and lingo are explicitly reflected back to him, your messaging will go in one ear and out the other—no sale for you.

Use windows to attract window shoppers. Use mirrors to attract customers—but make sure those mirrors reflect *them*, not you.

Bad Brands Bounce Sales

Do you know exactly what your sales reps and channel partners are pitching to potential customers? Trust me, you don't. You'd be surprised. Or, maybe not.

Mostly, they make it up as they go along: Your brand is so weak, confusing, or unfathomable (just look at your homepage) that it doesn't work in a sales call. If you have 1,000 reps on the street, you have 1,000 different brands.

Remember: Every time your salesrep opens his mouth, he's branding your company. What is he saying?

Commissioned reps are coin-operated, transaction-oriented machines. For the most part, each will do and say what works to close sales. Wouldn't you? The weaker your brand, the more your salesreps will assert themselves as your branding agents. Chaos, and branding failure.

Imagine that you're an energetic salesrep, armed with product training and imbued with HQ's brand du jour, sitting before your prospect. When asked to explain your company's value proposition (brand), you reflexively blurt out the slogan affixed to your company's homepage: *We take you to the cloud.* Bewildered, your prospect, neither meteorologist nor bird nor balloonist, flashes a blank stare. Bad news: Your pitch just bounced back.

This revenue-killing ordeal is akin to sending an ambiguously worded e-mail: The recipient either ignores it or bounces it back by initiating an exasperating, multiple-volley clarification exercise—ultimately ending in a heated phone call.

Lesson: Failure to hit and stick to your target on the *first* attempt—in an e-mail, during a sales call, or via a homepage—is an unacceptable, preventable error that carries with it high resource and opportunity costs.

A top salesman succeeds because he knows which words work. He speaks customer-centric language, not vendor-centric jargon. He'll try the "official" corporate message *once*; if it fails, he'll invent his own version. Every other sales rep will do likewise (one brand/salesrep), needlessly boosting the cost of sales, relegating the HQ-articulated brand to the trashbin.

Jargon, like a tennis ball, is fuzzy and hollow, and bounces off its target. Why? It's vendor-centric argot; customers reject it. They care only about *their* agendas, *their* lingo, and *their* pressures—not those of suppliers. Despite this, most suppliers are jargon junkies.

Steve W. Martin, who teaches sales strategy at the USC Marshall School of Business, knows that perceiving and leveraging customers' emotions—garnering GutShare™—is essential to successful selling. Cerebral selling, consequently, doesn't work; that's why mindshare—an absolute waste of shareholder capital—is meaningless and begets bad brands.

Martin penned an article in *Harvard Business Review* called "Seven Personality Traits of Top Salespeople." In trait #3, Martin explained the art of selling (emphasis mine):

> *Top sales performers seek to understand the politics of customer decisionmaking. They strategize about the people they are selling to and how the products they're selling fit into the organization **instead of focusing on the functionality of the products themselves.***

Selling to one is like branding to many but on a smaller scale, although the skillsets of the people involved are vastly different—unfortunately. Each endeavor requires constructing a detailed map of needs, emotions, politics, and behaviors—and then adeptly incorporating these "coordinates" into customer communications. This sounds simple, right? Evidently not.

Why such a big disconnect between how top salesreps and homepages (from marketing departments, PR firms, ad agencies, and Web developers) articulate value?

- Lack of communications competence (bad now and growing worse): Today's college graduates—the

OMG/LOL/BRB crowd—have no clue how to speak or write;

- Using impotent, consensus-driven committees, which excel at converting arrowheads into tennis balls;
- Strong aversion to being unique: Most people prefer to blend and imitate;
- Ignorance of human emotions and behaviors;
- CEOs assigning *low* priority to unique, jargon-free, GutShare-garnering branding.

This value-articulation disconnect explains perfectly why HQ-driven homepages invariably focus on product functionality, feature indecipherable jargon and forgettable slogans, and resemble complex cockpits—with switches, dials, and gauges; impossible to grasp or navigate; homages to products & designers, instead of customers—the keys to bouncing sales.

A top salesrep, alternatively, operates on a completely different wavelength: He relieves the pains and buttresses the ambitions of the execs in the decisionmaking unit—a far cry from "selling products"—by immersing himself in each one's politics and psyche. Speaking customer-centric language, rarely found on homepages, is paramount to his success.

I've asked many sales VPs what role their companies' homepages play in closing business. Typical reply: It plays no role; my salesforce ignores it, and our customers don't even look at it (see Branding Basics). A wasted strategic asset. Are you listening, shareholders?

When your customers and salesforce bounce your homepage, you have a bad brand—one that's synonymous with ambiguity, complexity, confusion, imitation, and insularity—keeping your company stuck in the white noise, indistinguishable from its competitors.

Does your brand stick or bounce? Quick test: If your top salesreps, who are great proxies for your customers, are pitching with their own arrowheads, it bounces. Getting the point?

CHAPTER TEN

Delusory Demand Generation

Corporations, hungry to increase top and bottom lines, are always on the hunt for ways to streamline the process of attracting prospects, converting them to customers, and retaining them as repeat customers. Some CEOs have deployed marketing-automation software for this purpose, with mixed results.

Consultant David Raab forecasts that vendors of marketing-automation software will realize $750M in 2013 revenues; he predicts slow industry growth—mainly because the software is too generalized for all companies and doesn't cure enough of their marketing woes.

One key component of marketing-automation software, the front end, is *demand generation*. To promote and explain the workings and virtues of demand generation, its purveyors and specialized industry consultants offer videos, seminars, webinars, and white papers. In my experience, whenever a product spawns a seminar industry, its value is questionable, at best.

So, exactly what is demand generation? According to Eloqua, a marketing-automation vendor and relatively recent Oracle acquisition, demand generation is:

> *... the art and science of creating, nurturing, and managing buying interest in your products and services through campaign management, lead management, marketing analysis, and data management.*

> Replacing actual human behavior with "Digital Body Language," Eloqua adds: *Today's buyer acquires [his] information online, through various sources, on a timeframe that makes sense to [him]. Because of this, marketers must focus on understanding the needs of the buyer and facilitating [his] buying process,* **rather than pushing marketing messages at [him].**

Marketo, also in the marketing-automation industry, defines demand generation thusly:

> *... the evolution of traditional lead generation and an important subset of inbound marketing. Unlike traditional programs that throw any lead over the wall to sales, it is about qualifying and prioritizing prospects, nurturing a steady crop of qualified leads that want to engage with sales, aligning marketing with sales, and measuring and optimizing the results over time.*

This all sounds pretty cool, doesn't it? There's one problem: demand generation is an illusion, a delusion; it doesn't and can't exist. In fact, it's oxymoronic.

NEWSFLASH: Demand generation is oxymoronic.

The dictionary definition of generate: to bring into existence; cause to be; produce. A marketer **can't** bring demand into existence, cause it to be, or produce it—i.e., "generate" demand. It seems the bloke who coined this oxymoronic term never made a face-to-face sale, which requires skills in attracting, qualifying, gauging, persuading, and negotiating.

In this impersonal age of text messaging and social media, human disconnection rules. The art of direct, genuine communication is dying; knowledge of human emotions is rare—clearly reflected by the jargon and technologies companies employ to engage prospects.

The vendors above assume they either can create (generate) demand, or that it simply will materialize if enough buying levers exist. Following that, the strategy is to use automation, akin to an assembly line, to manage and measure the lead-to-sale process.

Demand neither simply materializes, nor can anyone generate it.

Eloqua disdains "pushing marketing messages" at customers, admonishing marketers to focus instead on understanding their needs. Seriously? An arrow without an arrowhead? The brand (marketing message) *is* the arrowhead. How else can one hit the target?

This common error—discounting or disregarding the brand—is precisely the problem: It repels demand, is the seed of white noise, and no technology can fix it. Only those few who understand customers' needs and are proven wordsmiths can fix it.

Message Always Pulls Megaphone

Without a strong brand (marketing message), what will attract customers? If you think it's your product, think again. Of course, there's always that option to build an overly expensive salesforce, whose members will invent their own marketing messages—to your detriment.

Most firms, regardless of industry, look alike because their so-called "marketing messages" fail: they're jargon-filled, unfathomable product statements, which turn off customers. A bad marketing message (brand) is verification that the marketer behind it neither understands customers' needs nor how to articulate them.

Here's a common example of a bad brand (marketing message): *We make the fastest, cheapest, smallest, most-ubiquitous, easiest-to-use widget in the world.* The table below analyzes the brand's attributes. You should perform the same analysis on your brand.

BRAND ATTRIBUTE	YES	NO
Unique?		X
Evocative?		X
Succinct?		X
Memorable?		X
Repeatable?		X

Customers loathe and reject such typically generic, unimaginative white noise—causing them to view vendors alike and products alike, and make price-driven purchases.

Rather than fix bad messages, many marketers default to social media and email blasts—nonsensical and a huge mistake: sending white noise through a megaphone begets louder white noise. On the other hand, strong marketing messages (brands)—*which the audience can grasp in 15 seconds*—can articulate customers' needs, in their language, and *are the key to attracting them.*

In *The King's Speech*, Colin Firth deftly portrayed King George VI, whose speech impediment rendered him almost unable to communicate to his British subjects. The entire movie (a true story) was about his struggle to overcome this problem. His solution was *not* to improve PA systems, microphones, or the radio network; it was to improve his speaking skills. Message *always* pulls megaphone, just as horse always pulls cart.

Words Matter

In 1989, I wrote "The Mystery of Marketing," in which I asserted:

> *A market is akin to energy: it can be neither created nor destroyed. Marketers don't have that power, although many think they do. The best marketers can do is discover, ignore, cultivate, exploit, manipulate, anticipate, excite, compete for a market, but never create it. Why? Because a market is people: their money, logic, and emotions. They already exist.*

Like energy and markets, demand already exists. One can anticipate, discover, stimulate, cultivate, channel, and compete for demand—but never create (generate) it.

Words matter. Words dictate attitude, focus, and activity.

Those who wrongly believe that a product is a market will focus on—you guessed it—the product. Likewise, those who hubristically believe they can create demand will focus on the product and fail at branding. *Producting and marketing are mutually exclusive.* Attitude begets activity.

The way to fix demand generation is to scrap it altogether. Demand already exists; the best you can do is to "guide" it in your direction—no small task.

> **NOTE:** Those surgically attached to keyboards and obsessed with social media never will grasp this axiom, *so don't put them in charge of branding.* Digital body language? Are you kidding, Eloqua?

Replace "generation" with stimulation or cultivation, or both. Demand stimulation/cultivation. World of difference! Afterwards, you can create a brand *based on customer needs.*

Eliminate impersonal, *anti-*social, demand-repelling technologies, including marketing-automation software, if your employees are using these technologies as excuses for becoming detached from your customers. Don't be a blind tech-trend follower.

Finally, words matter. Using the right words—market, industry, stimulation—in the correct instances will drastically shift your company's attitudes, focus, and activities. Who benefits? Customers and shareholders. Nothing else matters.

CHAPTER ELEVEN

Pitching to Investors

Pitching is the art of articulating your brand (value proposition) in 15 seconds to your audiences—customers, investors, analysts, and media—so that they'll find it unique, compelling, memorable, and repeatable.

Many argue that every company must craft a different pitch for each audience, especially the investor audience. I fervently disagree.

Your brand is your brand is your brand: you have *one* value proposition, period. Consistency and uniformity, across all audiences, are crucial to your success.

Private Equity

Private-equity investors seek either to launch startups or restructure existing companies, with liquidity events as the ultimate aim. The diagram below illustrates that any entity—a single firm or a team of firms—must exhibit a strong brand to receive funding quickly. And, that brand must resonate with the capital sources, those executing the transaction, as well as the financial analysts (and journalists) who bless the deal.

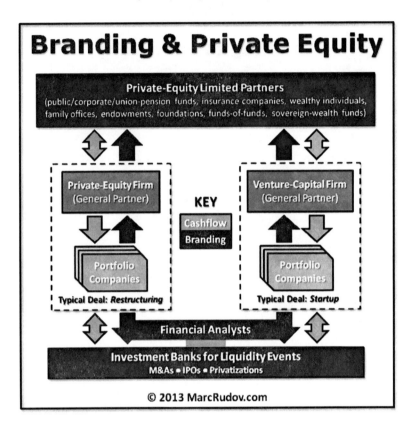

Common Freaking Sense

Here's pithy news that didn't shock me at all: About 75 percent of American venture-backed firms fail, according to the findings of Shikhar Ghosh, a senior lecturer at Harvard Business School. This failure record is three times higher than what's usually reported, a dismal track record no sports team would tolerate. Not only astounding, it's avoidable.

With proper branding, as the figure above illustrates, startup CEOs would see their success rates skyrocket. Alas, venture capitalists (VCs), their financial backers, don't require proper branding. Worse, they don't even know why they should require it: VCs are blind to branding.

I've had countless discussions—almost all wastes of time—with VCs about sharpening the brands of their portfolio companies (aka startups). This action, I posit, will boost the IRRs—annualized rates of return on the investments in their portfolio companies: If customers quickly grasp a company's reason for being, its visibility rises while its cost of creating that visibility drops, thereby spiking its value.

Common freaking sense, right? One would think. Yet, VCs mostly ignore it. Many of my colleagues around Silicon Valley share the same head-scratching experience. What's going on? I offer three explanations:

1. **VCs aren't incented to fix faltering companies:** VCs manage venture funds—capital from pensions, college endowments, and wealthy families—which they invest in their startups. VCs cash in by hatching these startups, after years of nurturing them, via IPOs or acquisitions. One homerun like Google can take them far. They also make money, even if most of their portfolio companies fizzle, via management fees collected every quarter—typically 2% of the total money in their venture funds.

2. **VCs are incurable jargon junkies:** VCs ride and milk technology waves, regardless of merit. The more jargon, the better. Hype has no limits. Why so many "social" startups, which look identical? VCs encouraged and funded them, despite not solving any real problems, then mesmerized the true believers at industry conferences. Branding, shmanding: it's all about the wave.

3. **VCs know little about branding:** You'll find some version of this cliché on every VC's homepage: *We invest in the best people creating companies in high-growth sectors of the high-tech industry.* Boring, forgettable, generic. Accordingly, VCs beam with pride when their startups, in turn, perpetuate forgettable generic jargon in *their* verbal and written communications: 4G, cloud, social, SaaS, LTE, Big Data, etc.—more branding blindness.

Harvard's Shikhar Ghosh found that three of every four VC-backed companies fail. I know why: VCs fail to demand strong brands from their portfolio companies. I've seen it firsthand. Limited partners—the investors in venture funds (see the figure above)—should be outraged.

VCs, it turns out, *do* need to sharpen the brands of their startups. Riding hyped tech-waves is *not* a panacea for branding. VCs must fund only those companies that solve real problems: Not knowing where my "friends" are or what they think about the minutiae of life is not a real problem.

CEOs can't succeed by spewing jargon, looking and sounding like every other company, and riding tech waves. They must offer value and solutions, not technology, and communicate to customers, investors, analysts, and reporters with unique, memorable, repeatable messages. Finally, CEOs must invest in solid branding counsel at *every* stage of growth—counsel typically not forthcoming from VCs.

To cure branding blindness in venture capital, the VC community must remove the hype-colored glasses. Success is *not* about the "wave," the technology, or the generic jargon. It's about the brand, the value proposition.

Why Should We Capitalize Your Business?

The key to quick capital-raising is answering, with ease and brevity, the fundamental investor question: *What is your business, what makes it unique, and why should we capitalize it—versus others?* The murkier your reply, the more protracted, difficult, and costly is the capital-raising process.

In the case of merger or acquisition, you want the acquiring company to make as rapid and easy a decision as possible. A similar question arises: *What is your business, what makes it unique, and why should we buy or subsume it—versus others?* Again, the murkier your reply, the more protracted, difficult, and costly is the M&A process.

Pitching to investors is, obviously, a time to prove strength of brand. When investors hear a pitch, they want to know how much money you're going to make them *and how you're going to do it*—logistically and viscerally. The facts do *not* speak for themselves.

Sales Machine

In essence, you make money (IRR) for investors by creating a sales machine, driven by a strong brand (value proposition)—validated by a growing base of customers who can't get your product/service fast enough, and often enough, at a net profit greater than your cost of capital.

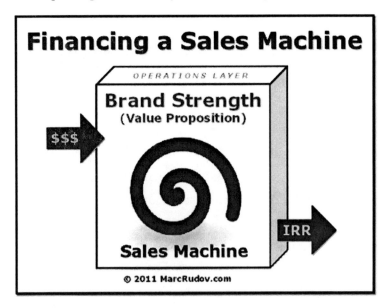

So, in the pitch, you must explain to investors the unique appeal of your brand. That's your focus—what they must absorb, along with understanding and accepting the operations required to deliver your *brand*.

Technology Is Subservient to Brand

As technology evolves, operational infrastructure must change to support the brand. Stated another way: *Technology is subservient to brand, not the converse.* Dependency on a specific technology or technological trend, and its concomitant jargon, therefore, is a huge mistake.

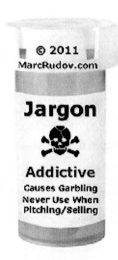

If your capital-raising pitch doesn't mirror your sales pitch, investors won't grasp why your company *should* exist.

Even if you miraculously receive funding from jargon-oriented, trend-obsessed investors, they'll be ineffective secondary salesmen. Why? A gaping inability to explain, in 15 seconds, the value you convey to customers—*the reason you're in business.*

Sending your investors into the world with a jargon-laced value proposition, therefore, is tantamount to branding failure.

Building Companies About Nothing

The Silicon Valley venture-capital firm (VC) is under intense pressure from its limited partners (investors) to fund as many startups, and ultimately earn as high a return, as possible. In this high-testosterone endeavor, each VC firm constantly races its rivals to discover, back, and launch the next Google.

Accordingly, VCs are spread so thinly, sitting on too many boards, that they have neither the time nor expertise to thoroughly screen entrepreneurs' ideas and business plans—instead allowing them to experiment and fail multiple times until something sticks.

In addition to being financially suboptimal, these rapid-fire, mulligan-oriented transactions kill something critical: branding. In fact, branding is extinct in Silicon Valley.

Branding is the art & science of articulating a jargon-free value proposition—*before building a product*—one that people react to, remember, and repeat. Alas, Silicon Valley is awash in forgettable, indecipherable jargon and ephemeral trends.

Pivoting

On 04.26.12, Lizette Chapman penned a revealing piece in the *Wall Street Journal* about the latest trend in techdom: pivoting, another term for the jargon pile. Wrote she: *The founders who change products and markets between one and three times raise more money than those who don't, according to Startup Genome Compass of San Francisco.* This defies all logic.

Jeff Bercovici of *Forbes* amplified Chapman's article by characterizing this flavor-of-the-month trend as a "Seinfeld moment": building companies about nothing!

Pivoting is what a politician does: in chameleon-like fashion, he replaces yesterday's slogan with one that resonates better today—to raise cash and get votes. In essence, he stands for and commits to nothing, the antithesis of branding.

Because VCs are in such a funding rush, largely in preselected spaces like "social media" rather than according to what consumers *actually* want and need, startups are no longer expected to know what products to build. Instead, they assemble teams and rent offices, then figure out the rest, on the fly. Huh?

What happened to doing your homework BEFORE starting a company, aiming before firing? That's so yesterday. Perhaps VCs have too much of other people's money to chase too few good ideas. Just sayin'.

Imagine engaging an architect to design your house, approving his plan, getting financing, hiring the general contractor, breaking ground, then watching these folks "pivot" your plan—and your cash—to oblivion. You can't.

Tweaking is one thing, but completely and repeatedly changing course is another. Yet, this is Silicon Valley's current MO—and why branding is extinct here, and why nebulous cloud computing originated here.

Yes, some companies like Instagram—which was under two years old, had 13 employees, and never saw a penny of income when Facebook bought it for $1B—will make it via lucky pivoting, but most won't. Instagram had started out as a Foursquare-like check-in service called Burbn but pivoted to photo-sharing. In fact, VCs are teaching prospective entrepreneurs to fail by becoming companies about nothing.

The only way to convince another that your company is about *something* is to believe it yourself, with conviction and PROOF that you're solving a real problem—for someone who *doesn't* live in Silicon Valley.

If, however, you pivot three times after raising seed capital, to attract more capital, you don't know and never knew your purpose—other than to get the VC's check.

So, what will you do, now that you have the cash: pivot three more times until nobody can fathom your reason for being? Cisco did this, then had to cut 10,000 jobs before getting back to basics. Cisco ignored the fundamentals of branding at great cost to its shareholders and employees.

Branding is extinct and won't appear any time soon—unless and until Silicon Valley ceases to operate by the current VC-driven model.

Ditch the Elevator Pitch

No entrepreneur can get through a day without someone, especially a potential investor, asking, *Do you have an elevator pitch?* This, for the unenlightened, is a company description so concise that one can deliver it effectively and persuasively to a fellow elevator passenger before he exits to his floor.

A few questions to ask yourself: Is the elevator journey one floor or 100? Can your ad-hoc prospect focus in an elevator? Do the other riders want to hear you talk? Are unknown competitors or journalists present to take advantage of your comments or the way you deliver them?

The elevator pitch is a total farce; stop trying to create and perfect it.

Articles abound on elevator etiquette. Why? Because riding in an enclosed box with strangers makes people feel awkward and unsure how to act. Some are claustrophobic and fear a service breakdown. They want space, silence, anonymity. They stare at their shoes, at the ceiling, at the floor indicators. Mostly, they want to get the hell out of there, as soon as possible.

Simply, *nothing* about an elevator is conducive to persuasion—ironically, the point of the elevator pitch. The very word *elevator* causes discomfort. Why would one use it, then? Words matter. To visualize yourself describing your company in an awkward, success-limiting situation is to defeat your confidence and creativity.

Why is visualization relevant here? It's key to success. Author and businessman Harvey Mackay, in "See It, Believe It: Success Starts in the Mind's Eye," notes that high achievers—including himself, Jim Carrey, Oprah Winfrey, Jonas Salk, and top Olympic athletes—always visualized success before realizing it. To visualize a dysfunctional scenario, therefore—pitching your company in an elevator—is a losing concept. Failing in your imagination is a bad start.

According to lore, the origin of this flawed metaphor, the elevator pitch, is Hollywood, where hopeful screenwriters would pitch to unsuspecting producers in elevators. Although its objective, speedy persuasion, is well-intentioned, it fails miserably: Most homepages, where company messaging must capture attention, are *totally unfathomable*. Yet, unwitting people enroll every day in elevator-pitch seminars. Waste of time and money. Seriously.

Elevator + pitch is a bad combination. Ditch it.

Ultimately, your pitch is your brand—*the unique, concise, pithy, jargon-free, memorable, repeatable articulation of your value proposition*—for audiences in comfortable venues. People don't perform or respond well in uncomfortable situations. Sustainable persuasion occurs *only* in comfortable situations.

Create the Banquet Pitch

When creating your pitch—an articulation of your brand, not your product—imagine sitting at a banquet table at a professional seminar. Most banquet tables are circular and seat 8-10 people. It's common for people at a banquet table to introduce themselves, in order. The next utterance is always the same: So, what does your company do? If your answer is, *We're a widget manufacturer*, you've failed the branding test.

You'll know you've created a strong brand when the people at your table "get it" in 15 seconds, without lengthy follow-up explanations. If you get blank stares and/or "What do you mean?" you have a problem. And, what you say at this banquet table should be identical to the messaging on your homepage: If it fails there, it fails everywhere.

The question is, *Who* should create/perfect your pitch? You need a proven wordsmith, whose words are memorable, repeatable, and evocative. If that's not you, *you're not the right person*. If you don't currently employ a wordsmith, don't wing it. Hire a qualified professional. Mediocrity is expensive. As Dirty Harry Callahan (Clint Eastwood) said in *Magnum Force*: "A man's GOT to know his limitations."

In an episode of *Seinfeld* ("The Beard"), Jerry met a pretty lady cop, who asked whether he'd ever watched *Melrose Place*. Jerry denied it. She knew he was lying and challenged him to a polygraph test. Jerry accepted, knowing he'd fail, and became increasingly nervous as the hour of judgment drew near. He asked his friend George Costanza (Jason Alexander), an expert liar, for advice:

> **JERRY:** So, George, how do I beat this lie detector?
>
> **GEORGE:** I'm sorry, Jerry, I can't help you.
>
> **JERRY:** Come on; you've got the gift. You're the only one that can help me.
>
> **GEORGE:** Jerry, I can't. It's like saying to Pavarotti, "Teach me to sing like you."
>
> **JERRY:** All right, well I've got to go take this test. I can't believe I'm doing this.
>
> **GEORGE:** Jerry, just remember: It's not a lie... if you believe it.

Jerry *did* take the polygraph test. He failed it.

Eliminate "elevator pitch" from your vernacular; it's worthless junk, a farce. Your job is to create/perfect a strong, jargon-free banquet pitch. You *will* meet potential investors, and customers, at a banquet table—and you must be ready, willing, and able to pitch them there.

Know your limitations. If you're not a wordsmith, hire one. Social media won't fix a weak brand—nor will search-engine marketing and vacuous news releases. Even if he were alive today, Pavarotti could not teach you to sing.

It's not a brand, just because you believe it is.

CHAPTER TWELVE
Pitching to Reporters

Consider the main job of a magazine or newspaper reporter/editor, news-Website reporter/editor, or radio or TV producer: *reporting news*. These media pros are in constant need of original content, something *newsworthy* to report.

Many, many CEOs are guilty of blanketing the world with what they believe are news releases—but are actually activity announcements. Often, the release-obsessed CEO is getting pressure from his board to move the Dow Jones or NASDAQ needle, thinking that all visibility is value. Wrong.

Alas, your itch to announce a new product or product update is of no concern to someone responsible for reporting news! Inherent in her decision to publish or broadcast any morsel of info: *our audience will care about this.*

Just because you're excited about your company's new widget doesn't make it news or newsworthy to the rest of us. The main question you must answer every time you want to open your corporate mouth is: *Who cares, and why?* If you can't answer that, objectively and honestly, you have no news.

It should occur to you that pitching reporters is akin to pitching customers and investors: it's about *brand*, not about you. *Isn't brand about me?* you ask. Already you've forgotten. Brand is value proposition—it's about *them* (customers, investors, and reporters), not about you.

Read one of your recent news releases. Pretend you're a customer or prospect. Do *you* really care about the words on those pages? Do *you* **react** viscerally to them? Will you **remember** them? Will you **repeat** them to others? Do *you* want to buy your product? I'll bet *no* to all questions above.

Imagine being a reporter who gets thousands of these bland propaganda pieces every day. It's mindnumbingly frustrating. Here's a shocking media axiom: Be unique or be ignored! Whoever makes a producer's job easier by submitting *news*—unique, concise, provocative, memorable, repeatable—will score with coverage. What a concept.

Bill O'Reilly asks his viewers every night to write to him. His instruction: *keep it pithy* (which means concise and forcefully expressive). No kidding. Sometimes O'Reilly adds: *We get thousands of letters every night. Our staff looks at the headlines in your emails. If they stand out, if they're concisely written and provocative—we like provocative—we'll read them. Otherwise, we'll throw them away.* Bill's a visibility expert.

O'Reilly's admonition is precisely the advice I'm giving you about your news releases. Read about my success with news releases in the *Word of Mouth* chapter.

CHAPTER THIRTEEN

Channel Branding

Companies employ direct and indirect channels for sales, influence, and distribution. A direct channel belongs to the company—a direct salesforce is comprised of company employees. Indirect channels consist of third-party firms that operate in either nonbinding alliance with or under monetary contract to the company. In either case, you, the CEO, must ensure that your business-development folks align with other entities that have brands compatible to yours. Why? Because conflicts cause chaos and loss of control.

If Your Dealers Stink, You Stink

Many execs *incorrectly* refer to channel partners as customers, and this is part of the problem: *channel partners are not customers*. Channel members are *business partners*, proxies, charged with doing your company's jobs: selling, conveying products and customer service, and buttressing your brand, to customers. You must recruit, approve, and forever manage the ones most compatible with your business.

Picking low-quality, incompatible partners and failing to control them, therefore, will kill your brand. Disney's *Sorcerer's Apprentice,* starring Mickey Mouse, is a perfect metaphor for losing control of your indirect channel.

In Disney's animation, based on a German poem by Goethe, Mickey Mouse improperly casts a magical spell, attempting to emulate his absent sorcerer boss, to empower a broom to do his water-carrying chore. Like too many vendors, Mickey falls asleep and loses control of the broom, whose self-guided actions flood the house's basement.

Upon awakening to the rogue broom, Mickey panics, attempting to remedy the chaos by chopping the broom into pieces. But, unexpectedly, each piece becomes a whole water-carrying broom, completely overtaking Mickey's authority.

Eventually, the sorcerer returns home to find his basement submerged in water. He removes the spell, the water disappears, and he punishes his contrite apprentice.

A friend asked me to help resolve a situation with her broken tractor. The unresponsive, incompetent dealer who sold her the tractor—now out of warranty—was willing to take money but unable to fix it. After a lengthy period of disregard, I volunteered to bypass the dealer and contact headquarters directly. The ensuing exchanges are presented below:

> HQ's first response came from a woman in "customer care," via email, who announced that she had tossed the ball to our regional "service" manager.
>
> The regional "service" manager contacted me, also via email, after speaking to our lousy dealer, inaccurately regurgitating our problem and making a suggestion: find another dealer. Wow! He claimed to have tried to call me, but I had no voicemail from him, nor did he post his phone number in his email.
>
> Not surprised, I called the customer-care rep. After some irritating verbal volleyball, during which she thrice repeated her annoying *out-of-warranty-out-of-luck* mantra, she asked what I wanted her to do.
>
> **My response:** Find us a five-star dealer, not a one-star dealer, and pay this dealer to diagnose the tractor's problem. Then, once we know the problem, with

verifiable specificity, we will purchase the parts and labor required to fix it. We will not waste another penny guessing at the solution. Been there, done that.

Her response: *We don't know, and can't know, the quality of our dealers. They are independent and do what they want.*

My response: I can't believe what you just said. Your dealers are extensions of you. If your dealers stink, you stink. You *must* know how well they perform. You must manage them to represent you properly. We customers don't distinguish between a dealer and headquarters. Your reputation is at the mercy of your dealers. How can you operate this way? We will tell everyone we know—and there are many ranches and farms around here—never to buy your products.

Her response: I'll summarize your concerns and send them to my management.

This tractor vendor, an international giant, has no channel control. Its attitude and *in*actions are destroying its brand—unfortunately, a familiar scenario. This vendor stinks because its dealers stink. Its dealers stink because *it* stinks. A vendor *must* lead its dealers by example, by demonstrating value and driving that value through the entire channel.

By the way, because of my indignation and threat to spread the bad word around town, this tractor vendor met my demands. Now, I ask you, Should it have come to this?

In our politically correct, team-oriented, don't-offend-the-Millennials world, control is a bad word—and that's why few companies have it. But, as Mickey Mouse demonstrated above, losing control causes chaos, destruction, and anger.

The dealer, from your indirect channel, is an extension of you. Independence is unacceptable. Passing the buck is unacceptable. You must control your channel, or it will control you, drive your customers away, and kill your brand.

How to Run Business Development

As I noted at the beginning of this chapter, business development and channel management encompass recruiting, approval, and managing of strategic alliances, which run the gamut from marketing/sales to physical-distribution accords. Companies, ideally, make such arrangements with third-party firms that have complementary products, services, brands, business philosophies, and, often, superior access to desired customers—in other words, brand synergy.

Jay Samit, president of ooVoo, a social video-chat service, shared his partnering philosophy, mirroring the gist of this chapter, with the *Wall Street Journal* in October 2013:

> *"When we were trying to figure out how to launch digital music at Sony and compete with Apple, it was easier to partner with McDonald's—'Buy a Big*

Mac; Get a Free Track'—and McDonald's marketing, which reaches hundreds of millions of people. So, it's really been the success of partnering the entrepreneur with someone that's established in an aligned field."

Your *marketing organization* should run the business-development function, to create leads and lead opportunities for the salesforce. This is an inviolable rule.

Never allow your salesforce to get near business development—as so many CEOs do. Why? Salespeople aren't strategic; they're tactical, deal-driven, and coin-operated.

With monthly sales quotas to meet, salespeople aren't trained or motivated or incented to identify, recruit, and manage compatible, long-term partners. Salesreps in the business-development role will act rashly and randomly, and jeopardize your brand.

Alliance partners must have and maintain strategic brand synergy with your firm. It follows, then, that salaried people from your marketing organization—compensated to take the long view—must manage and, yes, babysit them, and terminate them when necessary. Also, business-development professionals *must* be street-savvy customer advocates with field experience, not ivory-tower geeks.

Never should anyone from your company ever say: *We don't know, and can't know, the quality of our dealers. They are independent and do what they want.*

CHAPTER FOURTEEN
Always Be Branding

Imagine a *successful* standup comedian repeating a routine that, the previous night, elicited puzzled looks and muted chuckles from the audience. You can't. He'd immediately massage his message, tweak his tempo, and punctuate his punchlines until the audiences roar—and subsequently convert their friends into his paying fans.

Branding is based on the same principle as performing: continuously testing & tweaking the marketing message (brand) until it resonates in 15 seconds with customers, reporters, and investors, who react by purchasing, writing about, and investing in the underlying product and/or company, respectively—and encouraging others to do likewise.

The key principle of success outlined above: *always be branding*. The recent JCPenney saga provides a great example of a company that ignored this principle.

In 2011, Ron Johnson left Apple to take the helm at JCPenney, which had become staid and stationary: its 2010 revenues of $17.8B were below the nearly $20B realized four years earlier.

Johnson immediately converted JCPenney into JCP, a flashy, upscale boutique store—and replaced undecipherable discounting with fair/square, always-low pricing.

Problem: existing customers didn't like JCP. No doubt, Johnson had to shake up the retail chain and needed a new breed of customer who would appreciate his changes.

Reality: the "desired" customer resisted shopping at JCPenney, because of its legacy, even with a new name JCP; traditional customers fled in droves.

It's impossible to execute an overnight, wholesale replacement of current customers with "better" ones. Sales dropped 25% in Johnson's first 12 months. Five months later, the board fired him and brought back the CEO Johnson had replaced 17 months before—a nonsolution.

Bottom line: Johnson never took the time to test and tweak Penney's new brand until it resonated with the new customer. He could have begun his rebranding push by offering always-low pricing *without* the hipster JCP moniker. A comedian like Frank Caliendo, known and liked for doing voices and impressions, can't suddenly switch to derisive political humor and expect his current audience to approve.

Recently, I attended a medical-technology event, whose exhibit floor featured 140 vendors. As I walked from booth to booth, I read and heard nothing but jargonized, product-

.centric messages. This is typical, by the way, and the antithesis of branding. When I asked booth personnel what makes their companies *unique*, vis-a-vis their competitors, they answered with more jargon, akin to using a brand extinguisher. If they don't know what makes their companies unique, how can customers or reporters or investors know?

People buy value solutions, *not products and technologies*. Are vendors paying attention? No. With rare exception, and CEO approval, they reflexively and endlessly pitch products and technologies, hoping somehow to cheat immutability.

This disconnect between branding **(react/remember/repeat)** and the cryptic argot that vendors unfailingly spew to the outside world is enormous.

Poor branding—which needlessly increases your costs of sales, media, and capital—is a giant, pervasive, universal problem that few execs recognize or want to fix. **HINT:** poor branding *always* includes jargon-laced, functional descriptions of products and gratuitous hyping of technology.

Corporate Breathing

I know in advance, before discussing branding with CEOs, the excuses they'll give me for avoiding or delaying the topic. These branding-avoidance excuses are both alarming and comical:

- We're too busy for that
- Our company is too small
- It's not a priority right now
- It's too expensive
- We did that last year.

Let me get this straight: communicating one's message crisply and memorably to prospects, reporters, and investors is something to avoid? *Really?* Is our comedian too busy to sharpen his unsuccessful routine? Is this not a priority for him? Is he too "small" to worry about it? Is it too expensive for him to fix his routine? Didn't he fix it last year?

In fact, there's *no* excuse for avoiding or delaying branding. Do you avoid breathing? Not if you want to live. Branding is corporate breathing; without it, the other systems—especially product development—malfunction.

Inviolable rule: always be branding. *Not* never be branding. *Not* sometimes be branding. *Not* branding when and if we get around to it. *Not* branding when our company is larger. *Not* branding when we can afford it. *Not* waiting for our branding season.

The fundamental tenet of sales training is: *always be closing.* It means that the one armed with a solution to a problem should be on perpetual alert for those who need his solution, so he can persuade them to purchase it. Successful closing requires two sets of skills:

1. Deftness in prospect qualification, psychology, and persuasion
2. Ability to articulate the product's value in the prospect's language.

Ironically, the same CEOs who avoid branding would fire salesreps who aren't continuously closing.

Often, a salesrep possesses neither the technique nor the content of closing: her technique is transparently pushy, her content cloudy. Predictable outcome: "the close" will fail or drag on, needlessly raising the cost of sales. Is this happening in your company?

With training, her technique (qualification, psychology, and persuasion) can improve. What about the content, the value proposition? If your company has a cloudy brand, she'll have to *wing it*. Winging it, unfortunately, is the rule in sales—because salesreps have no choice. Result: they torture your customers with technohype and jargon-laced, functional descriptions of your products—the opposite of what succeeds.

Continuous Obligation

Take an objective look at your branding platforms: homepage, brochures, tradeshow booth, 10K, S-1, annual report, executive summary, keynotes, sales training, sales pitches, etc. Are they rife with jargon, technology hype, and product worship? If so, you're not branding.

Customers, reporters, analysts, and investors are deluged with the white noise of me-too competition. Put yourself in their shoes. To them, the plethora of vendors and products appear indistinguishable and generic.

This is bad news for you, right? Yet, you probably perpetuate white noise by cranking up the vernacular volume. Why? Real communication is a lost art in our new world of *un*social media. We live in a, like, culture that, like, believes texting is, like, OMG, communicating, and posting photos on Facebook is, like, being social. LOL.

Good comedians are branding experts. People laugh at comedians' jokes when: 1) they identify personally with the jokes, 2) the jokes are unique and clever, and 3) the jokes are delivered memorably. Customers *don't* identify personally with jargon, jargon isn't unique or clever, and one can't deliver jargon memorably. If you're jargonizing, you're debranding.

Once again, branding is articulating a unique value proposition, within 15 seconds, so that customers, reporters, and investors react to, remember, and repeat it. Branding is not an extracurricular exercise. Branding is your number #1 priority, your continuous obligation.

If you want your salesreps to "always be closing," you must **always be branding**. More about this in Chapter 17.

CHAPTER FIFTEEN

Myopic Mobile Marketing

Because of text messaging and "antisocial" media, people—especially college graduates—can't even talk to each other in plain, grammatically correct English. When's the last time you, like, tried to, like, talk to a teenager, the CEO and parent of the, like, future? You're lucky to get a, like, grunt in response to any question.

Ironically, small children know how to communicate. Eavesdrop on them sometime; it's beautiful to watch—*they actually talk to each other.* Sadly, once these kids reach the age when they can use cellphones and computers, they lose their interpersonal skills.

These days, some folks can't even express themselves, via any means, save clicking "like" buttons. How does one, let alone a vendor, communicate to them? A society of passive automatons we have built.

Yo, phone, e-mail, and conversational etiquette are relics of the past, Dude.

So, where will you find employees with stellar branding skills? Where? Obviously, from a tiny, shrinking pool of great communicators. Here's the key question: *Who will understand them?*

Immutable Laws of Human Behavior

You're at a banquet filled with cacophonous chatter, barely able to hear the person on your right. It's time for the program to begin. The guest speaker ascends the podium as the master of ceremonies (MC) quiets the crowd, to give the speaker control of the audience.

Control of the audience. Complicated concept? Hardly. Yet, "the enlightened" have discounted it via blind infatuation with social media, believing that technology magically renders obsolete the immutable laws of human behavior.

Audience control, the antithesis of social media, is paramount to branding success. To wit, here's a confounding, self-defeating practice I see everywhere, every day: companies asking prospects to *leave* their Websites—their primary branding platforms—to "like us on Facebook and follow us on Twitter." Huh? Can you imagine a maître d' greeting you at the door with an invitation to *leave* his restaurant?

I've attended investor meetings during which the presenting entrepreneurs, obsessed with creating something, anything, in social media, pitched the most-absurd company ideas imaginable. They weren't trying to solve real problems; they were robotically riding flavor-of-the-month tech waves.

Social media are the online equivalents of noisy, uncontrollable rooms. Aren't we always eager to *leave* noisy rooms? At a noisy tradeshow, doesn't a salesman always invite his prospect to conduct business in a quiet room? The answer to both questions is, of course, yes. We can't function in noise; that's why Bose sells noise-cancelling headphones.

If noise is so disturbing, why would the Internet make it palatable? It doesn't. In fact, "social" noise disturbs and, ironically, isolates us. Stephen Marche wrote, in May 2012, in *The Atlantic*, that Facebook is making us lonely. So, isn't living with excessive noise *anti*-social behavior?

Indeed it is. In fact, there's strong evidence that people, increasingly, are either tiring of Facebook or avoiding it altogether—they want their privacy and silence.

On May 15, 2012, GM announced that it no longer would advertise on Facebook because the poor ROI didn't justify the expense. A year later, Sheryl Sandberg, Facebook's COO, convinced GM's CEO to try again. I'm unconvinced. The fundamentals aren't there: without a remote MC, how can GM can't get anyone's attention on Facebook? This is not a target-rich environment, not a good branding venue. In a culture afflicted with a mobile-social obsession, expect irrationality.

Here's the reality: Whether branding, speaking, selling, publishing, broadcasting, or entertaining, you need a captive audience. But, if you can't hold and control your audience—*the message to and response from your audience*—you are talking to yourself. **Lesson: More noise, less control**.

If you're employing a "social" medium, ask yourself: Is it an influence channel that I control? Does it sharpen my brand? Does it drive customers to my Website and cash register? If not, dump it. Don't do anything just to copy a fad.

You can't control your brand without controlling your message, which requires you to control your audience. You can't control any audience distracted in a noisy room. A speaker wouldn't tolerate chaos; a marketer shouldn't, either. This is what GM originally had decided.

Twitter is planning an IPO (initial public offering). There's one hitch: On October 3, 2013, Twitter admitted, in its IPO documents, that 5% of its subscribers are fake (I'll bet the real number is 3X that figure). Its value depends on having *real* subscribers. A few weeks before this, multiple sources reported that 55% of Barack Obama's Twitter followers are fake. Still wanna bet your company on social media?

If the data prove that your social channels work, *really work*, use them. If, however, they exist to justify your FOMO (fear of missing out) but are costly, time-zapping distractions, delete them. Try this: Focus on the one influence channel you *can* control: your Website. How? *Make it worth visiting.*

Perpetual Adolescence

In late July 2012, I was chatting at a cocktail party with a NASDAQ executive, teasing her about the "botched" Facebook IPO, which had occurred two months theretofore. I opined that Facebook's business is fluff, based on dysfunctional behavior—a heretical comment in Silicon Valley. If it were a real business, I continued, its stock would have at least recovered to the $38 IPO price (it was $28 that day and hovers around $49 almost 18 months later).

Then, this NASDAQ exec reinforced my point about dysfunction with a personal anecdote, telling me that her teenage daughter recently had wanted to invite some friends over for dinner. Mom counseled her daughter to call each of them. *Call them? No way! Who calls people?* Instead, the teen "invited" her friends via an impersonal announcement on her Facebook page. "And, what if your friends don't see the invitation?" Mom asked. "That's their problem," her daughter sniffed. Such an infantile exchange is no surprise, and it typifies today's entitled youth and coddling parents.

In 2007, Diana West penned *The Death of the Grown-Up: How America's Arrested Development Is Bringing Down Western Civilization.* West posited that Americans are in a state of perpetual adolescence, rooted in the '50s and '60s, and that the transition to adulthood does not end until the age of 34. At a Heritage Foundation book event, West gave some eye-popping stats to explain America's mobile-social obsession:

- More adults (18-49) watch the Cartoon Network than CNN
- Readers as old as 25 are buying young-adult fiction, which is expressly written for teenagers
- The average video gamester was 18 in 1990; now, he's going on 30

- The National Academy of Sciences has redefined adolescence as the period extending from the onset of puberty (12) to age 30.

Dr. Keith Ablow, a prominent psychiatrist, explains the mobile-social obsession, as well as its consequences, by claiming that we're raising a generation of deluded narcissists. Consider his assessment when you see teens hermetically attached to their phones—and want to brand to them.

Increasingly, according to several reports from the *Wall Street Journal*, people query their favorite social sites exclusively via mobile devices, so frequently that they're losing their communication skills, brain cells, social etiquette, and abilities to make eye contact. In South Korea, experts say that teens are suffering from "digital dementia." The University of Michigan studied Facebook users over a two-week period and, according to the study's leader, Ethan Kross: "Rather than enhance well-being, we found that Facebook use predicts the opposite result—it undermines it."

Mobile Mobsters

I call the addicted, addled, dysfunctional, demented users of mobile-social technology Mobile Mobsters. They are the least social humans ever to live.

Antisocial is the new social. According to new research by Carnegie Mellon University's Human-Computer Interaction Lab, our culture's pervasive mobile-social obsession is making people dumber. Man-on-the-street interviews, conducted by *Jimmy Kimmel Live*, Fox News Channel, TheBlaze, Media Research Center, and other outlets continue to prove that most Americans, always glued to their smartphones, are utterly clueless about politics, history, government, and basic economics.

Furthermore, according to an April 29, 2013, piece in *USA Today*, our coddled Millennial college graduates are so attached to their mobile devices, and detached from decorum, that they're unequipped for the workplace. According to HR execs, the Mobile Mobsters answer texts during job interviews. Worse, they bring their pets and parents to the interviews! How infantile.

Something is very wrong here. Yet, most corporate execs are embracing social media with blind, illogical zeal. In March 2013, IBM's CEO Virginia Rometty told the Council of Foreign Relations that "social software will become the 'new production line' to create value." Is this not a case of myopic mobile marketing? It is.

Why? Because Rometty is betting shareholders' cash on dysfunctional behavior; it makes no sense. How detached can people become from each other, and from reality, before they're unable to function? Anyone who brings Daddy or Snagglepuss to a job interview is already at the red line.

I have a few questions for Ms. Rometty of IBM and her colleagues at other companies:

- What kinds of "customers" are at the other ends of these mobile devices?
- What are their occupations?
- How will you brand to them?
- What will you sell them?
- Is the mobile-social trend you're riding sustainable; if so, based on what logic?

Mark Zuckerberg made a big splash, in early April 2013, with his introduction of Facebook Home, a vehicle for even-more social interaction and advertising on Android-based smartphones. It's been a dud: the Facebook Home-sporting "HTC First" phone price was cut from $99.99, with a two year contract, to just 99 cents—with the same AT&T two-year agreement.

What's up with that? Jon Xavier, of *Silicon Valley Business Journal* (04.05.13), believes Facebook Home has crossed the user-privacy threshold; Facebook users have rejected it. A welcome sign of maturation, perhaps?

Critical Thinking

Let's step outside the zone of mobile-social obsession to apply a dollop of critical thinking. There's no possible way to perform useful work on a mobile device; one needs a desktop or laptop computer for that. So, those in the Mobile Mob can't, realistically, earn high incomes.

Here are some fun facts about Mobile Mobsters et al:

- One in five Americans is on food stamps
- California no longer requires eighth-graders to take algebra
- Half of working college graduates hold jobs *not* requiring college degrees
- 60% of students who earned bachelors degrees in 2012 were saddled with an average of $27K in debt
- 36 percent of Millennials—young adults, 18 to 31— are living with their parents
- 15 percent of those aged 16 to 24 are idle—neither in school nor working

On May 20, 2013, Yahoo announced its intention to acquire Tumblr, the New York-based social-blogging service, for $1.1B. Why? To gain the under-30 crowd: the perpetual adolescents, the deluded narcissists, the Mobile Mobsters— the apparent Holy Grail of corporate America.

Shopping, texting, monitoring friends' whereabouts, and posting photos and the minutia of daily life are *not* wealth-building activities. Are Mobile Mobsters a sustainably profitable market, merely because they "gather" en masse in a few places? C'mon.

Now, what products and services can they afford, *on a sustainable basis*, and is it profitable to serve them?

I'm still having trouble wrapping my mind around Virginia Rometty's *social software as a new production line to create value.* It's impossible to yield sustainable value from customers who have little of it to impart. Evidence abounds that, the more time people spend in the mobile-social world, the more dysfunctional they become. You do the math.

Myopic mobile marketing is the illogical zeal with which CEOs use mobile technology to reach and brand to the under-30 crowd—rejecting reality about their astounding immaturity. Including mobile-social in the overall marketing mix can, in profitable situations, make sense; a bet-your-company focus, though, makes no sense. *Are you doing this?*

The question is, Whose mobile-social obsession is greater: that of idealistic CEOs or that of deluded narcissists? Tough to tell. Either way, obsession always *clouds* judgment.

On October 30, 2013, Facebook announced its 3Q13 results: $425M in earnings, compared with a loss of $59M the previous year. Revenues increased 60% to $2.02B, year over year. In after-hours trading, FB shares shot up to $56. Then, on the call with investors, the CFO admitted that teens have left Facebook in droves (apparently, they're congregating on Instagram, a Facebook company, and SnapChat). Stock price bouncing around $49 the next day. Who will keep Facebook going? Oh, I forgot: adolescence ends at 30.

You see, chasing Mobile Mobsters is a game, a myopic game, a silly game. If perpetual adolescents begin magically to grow up, Yahoo's ridiculous overpayment for an unprofitable Tumblr will look even more myopic—and silly.

CHAPTER SIXTEEN
Clouding Your Brand

The barcode transformed supermarket checkout in the '80s. Its primary benefit: increasing sales while decreasing the cost of sales. What a coincidence! That's the same benefit—and objective—of a unique, compelling brand.

We know what it's like to stand in a checkout line when someone is holding up the works—because the scanner is malfunctioning or a barcode is missing or incorrect. The cashier must manually enter each SKU on her keyboard, exponentially expanding the wait-time of the entire queue. The collective frustration is palpable, while the retailer's cost of sales immediately jumps.

The typical vendor throws industry jargon on its homepage and then expects us to read "About Us," watch a corporate video, or peruse a whitepaper to comprehend its reason for being—disrespecting our time. Newsflash: it is *not* incumbent on us to decipher your business; it's your job to explain it—in *our* language, in 15 seconds, on your homepage.

An effective brand, like a barcode, effects instant identification of a message in the "reader." When we, as readers, recognize and accept a brand, we feel the familiar "beep" sound of a supermarket scanner in our guts, and we want to make a purchase.

Conversely, when we don't "get it"—can't instantly grasp your brand—we dawdle or never buy, thereby lowering your sales and raising your cost of sales.

Recall the last time you were stuck in a supermarket queue, when the scanner couldn't read a barcode. Did you feel frustrated, that the store was wasting your time? Did you consider leaving the store? Remember this the next time you dismiss, downplay, or deprioritize the urgency of crystal-clear branding.

Branding Fog

When a product has value and utility, and its purveyor brands it properly, customers will grasp its essence and buy it instantly. If, on the other hand, a product's value is murky, and competitors with me-too products do little more than compound the fog, "educational" seminars begin sprouting like weeds to clarify the fog. I began writing in 2009 about my favorite example of this foggy branding: cloud computing.

For the unindoctrinated, the "cloud" is technospeak for the amorphous, nebulous blob that encompasses the Internet and its various working parts. When engineers draw network diagrams, they depict the vast Internet, literally, as a cloud.

John Gage, the fifth employee of Sun Microsystems (acquired by Oracle Corporation in 2010), is credited with coining "the network is the computer." Perhaps this was true for Sun salesreps, but do others share that self-serving view? With hackers invading America's electrical grid and the US Department of Defense, Federal Reserve System, Zappos, Amazon, Apple, Yahoo, Sony, Nokia, and Facebook sites, and with the NSA snooping on all online activity, maybe not.

Since the dawn of computing, there's been a periodic swing between remote computing, once called timesharing, and on-premises computing. Cloud computing is the latest incarnation of the former—with software, numbercrunching, network, and storage resources outside the customer's walls.

Ultimately, end-users will gravitate to the incarnation du jour that satisfies their selfish interests—the one they can understand, afford, and control.

Technologists, unfortunately, have an irrepressible urge to use their vernacular in branding, as if the whole world gets buzzed by buzzwords. We've seen this, for example, with Web 2.0, a concept nobody can define. No surprise there were lots of Web 2.0 seminars back in the day.

It matters not how "cool" cloud computing might be or how much it excites the vendors selling it. What matters is whether cloud computing makes sense to a large audience in 15 seconds. It doesn't, and the number of seminars explaining it is inversely proportional to its visceral appeal.

What's more unfathomable and indefinable than a cloud? Very little. Yet, Marc Benioff, CEO of Salesforce.com, began the inexplicable hysteria by using this cloud concept as a way to brand his company's online software. Eventually, the lemmings followed suit. How does this nebulous jargonizing help any potential customer?

A cloud is meaningless to people, fuzzy and unclear. A cloud is fog. Fog blocks our views of beautiful landscapes and causes shipwrecks, plane crashes, and car accidents.

Why, all of a sudden, will "cloud" become crystal-clear when computing is tacked onto it? In fact, it won't. This is a futile exercise in branding fog!

Unless customers see solutions messaged in *their* language, in *unambiguous* terms, they will resist or ignore them. Should anyone have to attend a third-party seminar to understand your offering? Never.

Microsoft's Cloud

Throughout most of 2011, Microsoft ran a series of "to the cloud" commercials. These spots, featuring people in various stages of cloudgasm, made two fundamental branding errors: 1) selling "the cloud," which is meaningless, and 2) sending viewers three murky messages instead of a single crisp one.

The three messages in the spots were: cloud, Windows Live, and Windows 7—in that order. If we stop any of the spots after the actors send us to "to the cloud," we have NO clue about the advertiser's identity. We're already confused and distracted, instead of confident and focused.

To the cloud. What does that mean? Which cloud? Where can we buy the cloud? Is there a cloud store? We have no idea. The cloud is just a puffy mass of white noise to us.

Yet, Microsoft's initial salvo is the generic cloud message, and we don't know Microsoft is behind it. **Branding error #1**. Worse, almost every other tech vendor also speaks "cloud" lingo—except Apple, which had not yet released iCloud (keep reading).

Without offering a unique, gut-grabbing, memorable, repeatable brand, you have no hook and get no traction. Spouting generic technobabble is tantamount to wasting the shareholders' money—and the customers' time.

Was Microsoft showing us a problem scenario in any of these spots to which we, as business professionals, could relate? Sure. A few of them depicted execs connecting with geographically dispersed colleagues. No argument there.

Microsoft's solution? We don't know. There's this "cloud," whatever that is. Then, there's Windows Live, followed by Windows 7. So, what was Microsoft's message? And, how did its *three* messages interrelate? Microsoft expected *us* to decipher its brand. Not our job, Microsoft.

We neither have a gut reaction to nor remember Microsoft's three hazy messages: humans can't process three messages. Consequently, we cannot repeat the messages to our colleagues, because we have no idea what to repeat! **Branding error #2**.

Have you ever seen an archer use a trident? Doubtful. Such an act would be both aerodynamically and ballistically futile. Only a sharp, single-tipped arrow will fly, hit its target, *and stick to its target*. This is axiomatic in branding, too.

Yet, in communicating their brands—via homepages, speeches, ads, media appearances, and sales pitches—most companies use tridents instead of sharp, single-tipped arrows, believing that fatter ordnance yields better impact. They're wrong.

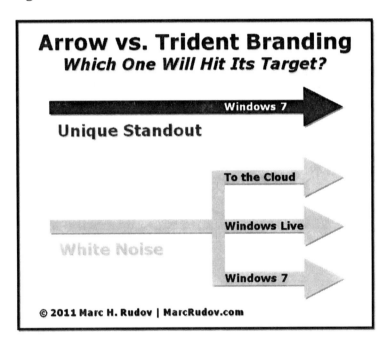

Had Microsoft simply stated its legitimate case— barriers to collegial connectivity raise the cost of our sales— and then offered *Windows 7* as the solution, we would have deemed Microsoft the unique standout for simply articulating our problem and offering us a clear, easy solution.

Instead, Microsoft sent us to the generic cloud—I don't recall requesting to be sent anywhere—the same ambiguous destination of its me-too competitors. Why, then, should we buy from Microsoft? We want a unique-standout vendor, not one stuck in the white noise.

Microsoft's singular goal was to get us to want and buy Windows 7, period. Alas, Microsoft blew it by clouding its brand in the cloud.

We don't care, or want to know, *how* Microsoft connects us to our colleagues—the technology will change again in six months. We care only that Microsoft *can* do it and explain it, simply—like hitting a bullseye in one shot.

At the end of 2011, Microsoft replaced these cloudy spots with a clear one showing a son helping his father punch up a sales-forecast slide using Windows 7. That's it. Simple!

Apple's iCloud

On June 6, 2011, Steve Jobs, having emerged briefly from his medical leave, made a rare branding blunder in a product announcement: incorporating "cloud" in its name. I was disappointed in him; really, I was.

Jobs heralded Apple's free iCloud service, which allows users to store remotely their music, documents, photos, and apps from their iPhones, iPads, and Macintosh computers.

As I've opined previously about cloud computing, using generic vernacular in branding is a major blunder:

1. Generic is the antithesis of unique
2. Nobody can define cloud
3. Every vendor under the sun *also* uses cloud:
   a. Amazon's Elastic Compute Cloud
   b. IBM's SmartCloud
   c. Dell's Cloud Computing
   d. Oracle's Cloud Solutions
   e. SAP's Cloud Computing
   f. VMWare's vCloud.

You get the picture. Are you confused? You should be. Confusion=CO$T. There's a reason every car is not called a Ford, right? When I hear cloud computing, in addition to its nebulous idiocy, I think of Wikileaks, Edward Snowden, NSA spying, and hacking. Putting all your assets online, because it's the thing to do, is an impetuous, foggy, risky decision—*the epitome of groupthink and blending.*

Adding insult to branding injury, by choosing iCloud as product name, Apple has milked all it can from the letter i, which, in a number of industries, is rapidly becoming as generic as salt. Some believe that sticking a lower-case "i" in front of generic vernacular makes it unique. Really? Look at the list of i-names in the following table, already in existence, unrelated to Apple:

NAME	INDUSTRY/DESCRIPTION
iCharts	Online portal of charts on any subject
iComfort	Serta's memory-foam bed product
iContact	Online email-marketing service
iDrive	Online-backup service
iGoogle	Google's customizable homepage
iHeart	Clear Channel's online radio streaming
iPage	Website hosting
iPower	Website hosting
iShares	BlackRock's ETF portal
iUniverse	Self-publishing portal
iVillage	Online portal for women

This blind cloud mimicry invokes Mark Wahlberg (as Charlie Croker) admonishing Edward Norton (as Steve Frazelli) in *The Italian Job*: "You've got no imagination." That's right. No imagination. Does Apple own *i*? No. Does Apple own *cloud*? No. So, how does *i* + *cloud* equal unique? It doesn't.

The morning after the iCloud announcement, I awoke to two local radio hosts discussing it. Inevitably, they asked each other the obvious question: *What's a cloud?* Bingo.

The *Wall Street Journal* reported iCloud's birth with an article entitled "Apple Opens Locker for Songs." Why locker? Locker is a word everybody understands. Duh.

Succumbing to peer and media pressure to copy your competitors by shoving generic buzzwords and vernacular into your brand is a colossal mistake—one that tech firms seem destined and delighted to make. Yet, even the mightiest brander of all, Apple, made it. That will be a cloud hanging over Cupertino for a long time.

Obsessive Cloud Disorder: OCD

In a now-famous session at OpenWorld 2010, that year's installment of an annual Oracle event, Larry Ellison, Oracle's CEO, struggled to define cloud computing to the audience of business execs and IT managers. I believe he felt pressured by his board to look "cool" and "with it" on Wall Street—one year after telling Ed Zander, former exec of Sun Microsystems and Motorola, at a Churchill Club dinner, that cloud computing is nonsense and water vapor. Larry's 2009 position was spot-on.

As you've been reading here, no jargon occupies the Silicon Valley lexicon more than cloud computing—except social media, mobile, and Big Data. Cloud has become an absolute obsession, and a ridiculous one at that.

The danger with obsession: The more one is fixated with something—whether a company, product, technology, or industry—the more blind he is to its folly. Sound familiar?

The OCD crowd ignores and rejects dissension. In 2012, I attended a tech conference in Silicon Valley, where "cloud" dominated the agenda and the narrative. Not one speaker on the roster debated cloud's detriments and drawbacks. *Not one detractor.* More like a religious revival than a logical business forum. We heard about public clouds, private clouds, and hybrid clouds. Huh? The lemmings in attendance left the event convinced that weaving cloud into their discussions and brands is a good idea. Nonsense.

What are the detriments and drawbacks of cloud computing? In case you've never asked this:

- **Confusion:** Nobody, outside the Silicon Valley bubble, understands this nebulous jargon—just ask a retailer in Lima, Ohio. Why cause customer confusion with vendor-speak?

- **Contradiction:** The word itself is the antithesis of stability and clarity. Anyone who's flown through a cloud knows that, unlike a steel vault, it is comprised of water vapor—intangible, ephemeral, amorphous, borderless. In social discourse, cloud *always* has a negative connotation (e.g., clouded judgment, cloud the issue).

- **Common:** The objective of branding is to convey unique, compelling, and memorable value. If every vendor uses the same generic, meaningless term— cloud—blending is the rule; building a unique brand is impossible.

- **Unsafe/Unwise:** Never put all your eggs in one basket—cloud computing does exactly that. Many sites have been hacked by pernicious individuals, groups, and governments—resulting in millions of passwords, bank-account numbers, and secret info stolen. Storms have disrupted other sites. Yet, the OCD crowd ignores the safety, reliability, and control of on-premises computing.

Since Larry Ellison, mentioned above, converted from cloud scoffer to embracer, no Silicon Valley luminary has publicly lambasted cloud computing—until Steve Wozniak, cofounder of Apple, called it horrendous. He averred: *"The more we transfer everything onto the web, onto the cloud, the less we're going to have control over it."* Bingo, Woz.

When articulating a value proposition—a brand—you must employ customer (not vendor) language. Technology is a means to an end, *not the end.* Your brand must be about value and benefits, not infrastructure. When buying a TV, does the salesrep lecture the customer about the PG&E grid? Not if she wants to sell a TV. Infrastructure is invisible; the TV buyer just wants to enjoy the Super Bowl.

Jack Dorsey, CEO of Square and chairman of Twitter, opined to *Fortune* in July 2012: *"To me, that is the pinnacle of technology—when the technology disappears completely."* Tell that to the OCD crowd, Jack.

Your "obsession" *should* be about customer value, not your delivery vehicle du jour, which will forever change. Let's say, for example, that you sell a backup service. This year, it happens to be an online service. What's its value proposition? *It can save someone's ass from the job-ruining humiliation of losing important files.* **That is what you say!** Maybe next year, because of rampant hacking scandals, you'll switch gears to sell an *on-premises* backup system, for the same purpose. What will change? The end, the brand (value proposition)? No. Just the *means* to that end. Same brand. Same messaging.

Do you now see the difference? Great! *That* is how to articulate value in customer language. *That* is branding!

Death of Nirvanix

In September 2013, the *Wall Street Journal* began reporting about the potential demise of Nirvanix. Then, on the 27th of that month, it ran this headline: "In a Blow to Cloud Computing, Nirvanix Officially Shuts Down."

Nirvanix, which began operations in 1998, declared bankruptcy on October 1, 2013, receiving approval a week hence. This company offered public, hybrid, and private cloud services—which, to me, are utterly meaningless terms, as I opined earlier in this chapter.

Here's what Deborah Gage wrote in her final *Wall Street Journal* article about Nirvanix (my emphasis added):

> Still, the sudden and secretive way that Nirvanix is shutting down has **raised questions about the future of cloud computing**. Nirvanix is the second venture-backed cloud-storage company to fail so publicly in less than three years—Cirtas Systems Inc., which had raised a little over $30 million, closed abruptly in April, 2011.

Despite the hype around cloud computing and the several cloud companies that have been successful so far, Nirvanix's sudden demise serves as a **warning once again to be careful about putting anything of value in the cloud.**

I have nothing else to say about cloud computing or using *cloud* in business articles, taglines, product names, company names, conference themes or advertising slogans. There's nothing positive or clear or intelligent about the word cloud in business. Stop using it.

CHAPTER SEVENTEEN
Lasting Impression

We've covered a lot of ground in this guide to branding. You now should have a solid grasp of and appreciation for the importance and priority of branding.

In the end, a successful brand leaves a lasting positive impression—*a unique, lasting positive impression*. According to Dictionary.com, an impression is *a strong effect produced on the intellect, feelings, conscience, etc.* What a coincidence! This is GutShare redux (see Chapter Two). The gut is where you move a customer, a reporter, an analyst, an investor.

Remember: mindshare is utterly meaningless; people don't make cerebral decisions or purchases. Delete mindshare from your company's lexicon. GutShare is gold.

Using jargon and product descriptions will earn you *no* GutShare and leave *no* unique, lasting positive impressions. It will, though, create white noise—and enable branding failure.

In prior chapters, I stated and reiterated that a brand is a value proposition the intended targets *react* to, *remember*, and *repeat*. A comedian's funny only if the audience laughs, right? But, realtime laughter isn't enough. He doesn't become golden until people can articulate his style, repeat his jokes at the water cooler, and share videos of his routines.

Your company is subject to the same rule. Your target audiences validate your brand when they can articulate your raison d'être, buy your product and rave about owning it, write about your product, and invest in your company—and have unique, lasting positive feelings afterwards.

In fact, without audience validation, your brand isn't yet a brand. Branding, in reality, is a continuous cycle of value-proposition articulation, approval, and updating.

Regardless of any plan or activity, in business or life, you face countervailing forces. Customers, analysts, investors, and reporters will reject or ignore your weak brand. But, if your brand resonates with targeted audiences, rivals will copy it—etching away your competitive advantage.

When Apple launched its first retail store in 2001— unique because of its open spaces—competitors and analysts threw rocks, *but customers flocked.* On October 15, 2013, Apple announced the hiring of Angela Ahrendts, CEO of Burberry, to head its retail and online sales, which have been in turmoil since Ron Johnson left in 2011 to become CEO of JCPenney. Johnson failed at Penney, lasting only 17 months there, because he tried to replace, overnight, the old customer base with a newer, hipper one. Traditional customers rejected his rebranding program and messaging. What happened to Apple's iconic stores? Copycat competitors, over time, have deflated Apple's unique balloon with their me-too stores.

The Branding Cycle

A few paragraphs ago, I refined my branding definition as a *continuous cycle* of articulating, getting approval for, and updating your value proposition. Let's visualize this.

In phase #1 of branding, as seen in the figure below, the vendor articulates its product's unique value proposition (UVP), which contains neither jargon nor product description. An example of a UVP: *we halve your labor costs without firing anyone* (notice the absence of jargon or product description).

In phase #2, the prospect receives the message, which resonates with her. She develops a unique feeling about the product and becomes motivated to buy it.

In phase #3, the prospect is now a product-using customer, who exhibits a unique feeling about owning it. The adept vendor will solicit customer feedback for analysis of her feelings and expressions thereof, to determine how or whether to update the original UVP.

This cycle, a fight to stay unique, continues as such over time. Any breaks or disconnects in the cycle can beget dilution, termination, or, worse, inversion of the unique, lasting positive impression.

Remember the example above of Apple's stores: The more successful your brand, the more rivals will copy it. You must be *endlessly diligent* in making your company seem unique to your audiences. You can't rest on your branding laurels, as companies frequently do.

Like Tuning a Piano

Yes, companies tend to rest on their branding laurels, sticking with weak brands that don't sell or with brands that once sold but no longer do. It's all-too common for a company to articulate and disseminate its brand, and then let it run like a wild horse. In other words, they execute phase #1 above, then quit. Why? Corporate politics, turf wars, egos, lethargy, and incompetence.

This is my only explanation for GEICO's unending onslaught of weird, inexplicable, inconsistent, unfathomable, torturous, irrelevant spots: an irritating brand about nothing ... and a giant waste of shareholder cash.

Letting a brand run like a wild horse is amateurish—even if it luckily, temporarily works—because audiences are fickle, distracted, inattentive, and mercilessly bombarded with indistinguishable competing brands.

Making audiences wade through this sea of white noise, by failing to continuously update, or tune, your brand, is an unforgivable, hubristic sin—resulting in minimized or delayed purchases, investments, and word of mouth, and increased costs of these lifelines, respectively.

A *good* marketer knows, in advance, when a brand will resonate with customers, investors, and reporters—through constant contact with them, visceral feel, and experience with previous campaigns. Besides, she can modify it over time through continuous testing and tuning, or scrap it if it falls flat.

In fact, branding is akin to a musical recital: there's no room for a tin ear. For those obsessed with and rewarded for managing audience satisfaction, the tuning regimen is a big part of daily life.

When experiencing the great virtuoso performances of Vladimir Horowitz, who died in 1989, one was struck not only by his style and accuracy but also by his piano's perfect pitch.

Had his music—his message—emanated from an out-of-tune Steinway, he would have irritated his audience, sullied his brand, and ended his career.

The tuning fork and piano tuner were, then, as integral to Horowitz's success as his skill. As Marshall McLuhan once said, *The medium is the message.*

According to Steinway & Sons: *No matter how expertly a piano is tuned, atmospheric variations and the nature of the piano's construction constantly conspire to bring it off-pitch. So, "set it and forget it" doesn't cut it.* Bottom line: always be ready to tune it.

By the same token, no matter how expertly your brand is tuned (or how expertly you *think* it is tuned), atmospheric (market and industry) variations and the nature of your brand's construction constantly conspire to bring it off-pitch. Again, "set it and forget it" doesn't cut it. Bottom line: always be ready to tune it.

Were Vladimir Horowitz alive today, can you imagine him appearing at Carnegie Hall, hoping and assuming that his piano is still in-tune since his last performance? Of course not. The medium is the message; it must be perfectly tuned.

When to tune your brand? Now. Tonight. Tomorrow. Always keep that tuning fork handy; your audience is listening—and your rivals are always copying. Finally, beware the discordant brand-killers: corporate politics, turf wars, egos, lethargy, incompetence—and anyone with a tin ear.

The Blending Impulse

To repeat what I stated in the second chapter: You, the CEO, must fight your "blending impulse" and that of your staff, because it *will* dilute your brand. *Branding and blending are mutually exclusive.* Standing out above the white noise of me-too competition might rattle your comfort zone (see Chapter Six), but that's what it takes to excite customers, investors, reporters, and analysts.

Too often, CEOs, and the blenders on their payrolls, believe the antidote to jargon is ... *slicker jargon.* Occasionally, you'll hear people say they should dejargonize, but they just can't bring themselves to do so. Rarely do employees, ad agencies, PR firms, or branding consultants get pushback from CEOs for using jargon. Why? *CEOs* use jargon and don't perceive a problem with it!

Result of no pushback against jargon? You guessed it: more of it, not less. Jargon dominates homepages, brochures, conference speeches, sales presentations, investor pitches, company meetings, PR, and advertising.

Jargon eventually becomes self-reinforcing and self-perpetuating, to the point that its creators and perpetuators truly believe everyone is in-sync with it. Wrong, wrong, wrong.

Branding Is Like Singing

Love him or hate him, Simon Cowell is a brilliant judge of singing talent. There was a time, many seasons ago, that I watched *American Idol*. Cowell admonished many hopefuls with this: *"I still don't understand what makes you unique!"* In a recent interview with HollywoodOutbreak.com about *The X-Factor*, the show he joined after leaving *Idol*, Cowell told the interviewer that one of the most important facets of being a successful singer is the ability to make a lasting impression on the audience: *"Being unique. Being remembered. Being focused."* Thank you, Simon Cowell.

Cowell's advice is timeless and applicable everywhere. Singing is like branding; branding is like singing—and, as we've seen before, like all performing. Making a lasting impression is everything. Notice that great singers know how to be unique—by their styles and music choices—and rivals have a tough time copying them.

With jargon, even slicker jargon, you *cannot* be unique, *cannot* evoke emotions, *cannot* leave a lasting impression, *cannot* have a powerful brand, and *cannot* lower your costs of sales, capital, and media. So, why are you jargonizing?

If they don't feel it, they won't buy it. There are *no* cerebral purchases.

CHAPTER EIGHTEEN

Final Thoughts

I promised in the preface that, by reading this guide, you would change your understanding of, attitude towards, and priority for branding—a true paradigm shift. I hope we now can consider this mission accomplished. You now know what branding is—and what it *isn't*.

As I stated upfront, branding is *your* responsibility, even though it is not your expertise and probably outside your comfort zone. As the CEO, you'll speak in front of customers, partners, analysts, investors, reporters, and TV audiences. What you say influences all of them. Accordingly, you are the brander-in-chief. You must *not* ramble on and on to these audiences in jargon, with paragraphs-long depictions of your company's raison d'être. You *must* have a unique, concise, memorable, repeatable pitch that makes a lasting impression in 15 seconds—and it must appear on your homepage and all other branding platforms. *If you don't have it, contact me.*

We've covered a lot of material in 17 chapters that I'm confident you won't get anywhere else—from definitions and concepts to why branding helps you avoid commoditization and boosts your bottom line to honest but politically incorrect discussions about branding fears, politics, and committees.

At this point, you are armed with the tools to revamp your company, eliminate jargon, end "producting," and engage in true branding by hiring the right people to articulate and convey the right messages.

Finally, after you've read and highlighted this guide, make sure that *all* your marketing people get their own copies to absorb. When you need additional branding help, call me. Good luck!

ABOUT THE AUTHOR

 Marc Rudov, wordsmith extraordinaire and inventor of GutShare™, is a branding and marketing consultant in the Silicon Valley area. He's headed marketing organizations in both large and small companies. Rudov is known worldwide for creating and articulating unique, concise messaging—through his writing, consulting, speaking, and media appearances—that audiences *react* to, *remember*, and *repeat*.

Mr. Rudov rails against industry, product, and technology jargon, and teaches his clients (most of whom are jargon junkies)—from various industries—to escape their comfort zones to brand in customer language. Moreover, Rudov insists the root of marketing (and branding) failure is rife misuse of the word *market*, which means *customers*, not products.

Rudov earned his engineering degree from the University of Pittsburgh and his MBA from Boston University.

Marc Rudov is available for radio & TV appearances, debates, speaking engagements, and, of course, new clients. Find him at MarcRudov.com.

CPSIA information can be obtained
at www.ICGtesting.com
Printed in the USA
LVOW12s0149050117

519796LV00002B/174/P